Yoga Calm® for Children

Educating Heart, Mind and Body

by
Lynea Gillen, MS, RYT
Jim Gillen, RYT

Twelfth Printing 2016

by Bang Printing

LCCN: 2007906569

ISBN 978-0-9799289-0-1

Published by:
Three Pebble Press, LLC
10040 SW 25th Ave
Portland, OR 97219-6325 U.S.A.

orders@ThreePebblePress.com
www.ThreePebblePress.com

Photography by Straub Collaborative, www.straubphoto.com
Book Design by m2design group, www.m2dg.com

Printed in the United States of America on acid-free recycled paper with soy-based ink.

To the memory of
Darin Noehren and Joan Gillen

Contents

Foreword

This book is much more than a yoga book: it's a comprehensive guide to understanding and guiding children in school in a way that looks at the whole child. How can we support children's academic success if we are not acknowledging the impact of physical and emotional conditions on their everyday learning? Even for teachers or counselors who are not incorporating "yoga" as such into the school day, this book is extremely useful for its guidance in dealing with the everyday emotional life of the child. Lynea and Jim provide many excellent ideas for handling specific situations as they arise.

Everything that is shared in *Yoga Calm for Children* rings true with my experiences with children in schools over the past twenty years. The ideas and insights go beyond the conventional wisdom to show how teachers can be some of the best providers of emotional support for students. Emotional guidance is, of course, such an important part of children's everyday education—and of their academic success. There is so much a teacher can do in the teachable moments that occur all through the day! The techniques and examples provided in this book can definitely equip teachers to feel more ready to provide emotional support. With knowledge, the entire school community can support development of the whole child, both in and beyond the classroom.

Chapter 5, with its illustrations of the poses, suggested length of time, variations and integration, and notes is quite simply the best of its kind that I've seen. Lynea and Jim clearly understand that the more specifics they offer us to practice, the more comfortable we can become as we evolve into our own style. Moreover, Lynea's personal stories set the standard for how we can respond compassionately from these principles and involve the whole school community.

This is truly an invaluable handbook that provides detailed and thoughtful information for counselors and teachers who want to incorporate the enormous benefits of yoga into a standard curriculum. It is also a beautiful expression of how, just by shifting the way we *are* with children, we can affect their lives.

Frances Douglass, PhD
School Psychologist
Seattle, Washington

Acknowledgments

We are so grateful for all the support, encouragement, and expertise that we received from our publishing team and our community of students, teachers, friends, and family in the process of writing this book.

First thanks must go to River Mill Elementary's students, staff, and parents, whose trust and belief in Lynea were instrumental in the development of Yoga Calm. We especially acknowledge Sue Dumolt and Larry Adamson, who provided encouragement during the early challenges, and Carla Austin and Eileen Gillen, who believed in the project from the beginning.

We would also like to recognize our teachers and mentors who taught us the skills that we are passing along in this book: Anne Bagwell and Joe Alexander for their great counsel; and Julie Gudmestad, Shari Friedrichsen, Diane Wilson, Anthony Bogart, SarahJoy Marsh, and Adeline Morris—our yoga teachers. Special thanks to Julie Gudmestad for her guidance on the breath and activity chapters.

We would like to thank our developmental editor, Lisa Verigin, for her skill and incredible patience with the process, and our copy editor, Judy McNally, for her exquisite attention to detail. We also extend our gratitude to Michael Marcheschi, friend and designer, who has an eye for elegance and beauty, and to David Straub, photographer and dear friend, who generously contributed all of the incredible photos in this book. Lisa, Judy, Michael, and David, you are a fantastic team. We couldn't have done it without you.

Finally, we would like to acknowledge Jim's siblings—Mary, Libby, and John—and Lynea's siblings—Paula, Becky, Shelly, Carrie, Jamie, and Christie— for providing emotional support during the writing of this book, as well as the following friends and students who listened to our stories, reviewed the manuscript, modeled for the book, fed us, supported us, and provided encouraging words when we needed them. Our love goes out to all of you.

Mary Faith Bonney	Alison Foraker	Elise McIntosh
Mary Ellen Bray	Don Francis	Tom Melling
Andrea Burke	Don Harring	Sean McCrary
Karma Carpenter	Carl Hay	Moana Musika
Emily Chavez	Diane & Peter Hower	Nick Olson
Jimmy Chavez	Julie Hurtubise	Paulette Rees-Denis
Lois Chavez	Jordan Jeffries	Tiffany Renshaw
Harriet Cooke	Devin King	Jude Siegel
Frances Douglass	Deborah Langford	Chari Smith
Claudine Ebel	Lacey Lasley	Jeff & Judith Sosne
David Ellman	Lindsey Lasley	Doug & Kathleen Verigin
Sarah Feldman	Lisa Lepine	Benjy & Heather Wertheimer
Kathy Flaminio	Madison & Sabrina Marcheschi	Tymmera Whitnah

A Note to the Reader

The book you are holding began as a handbook for the Yoga Calm workshops we teach both in Portland, Oregon, and around the United States. In developing the material, we have striven to keep the style and format simple and practical, knowing that those most apt to use this book on a regular basis will want and need to find specific activities and information as quickly and easily as possible.

To facilitate this, those seeking physical yoga activities, for example, can turn immediately to the activity pages in chapter 5, while those seeking social/emotional skill-building activities and relaxation techniques can turn to chapters 6 and 7, respectively. Chapter 9 puts all the activities together into sample class flows and recommended sequences for various classroom situations.

We have chosen not to interrupt the text to document the wealth of research that shows the immense benefits of yoga for children. For those interested in following up on that research—or just reading more about the issues discussed herein—we have provided a thematic bibliography. You can also learn more on our website, www.yogacalm.org.

Additionally, to give examples of how Yoga Calm works in actual practice, we have provided a number of anecdotes, set off in italics. These are all true stories taken from Lynea's years of teaching and counseling children, told in her own voice. In these stories and other references to children we have worked with, names and other identifying details have been changed to protect the children's privacy.

As you embark on your own journey of sharing Yoga Calm with students, we hope you will—and encourage you to—share your stories with us and others. It is through such sharing and learning together that we can nurture and support children ever more effectively, giving them the inner resources to live in ways that are beautiful and supportive of their own true natures.

— Lynea and Jim Gillen

Portland, Oregon

info@yogacalm.org

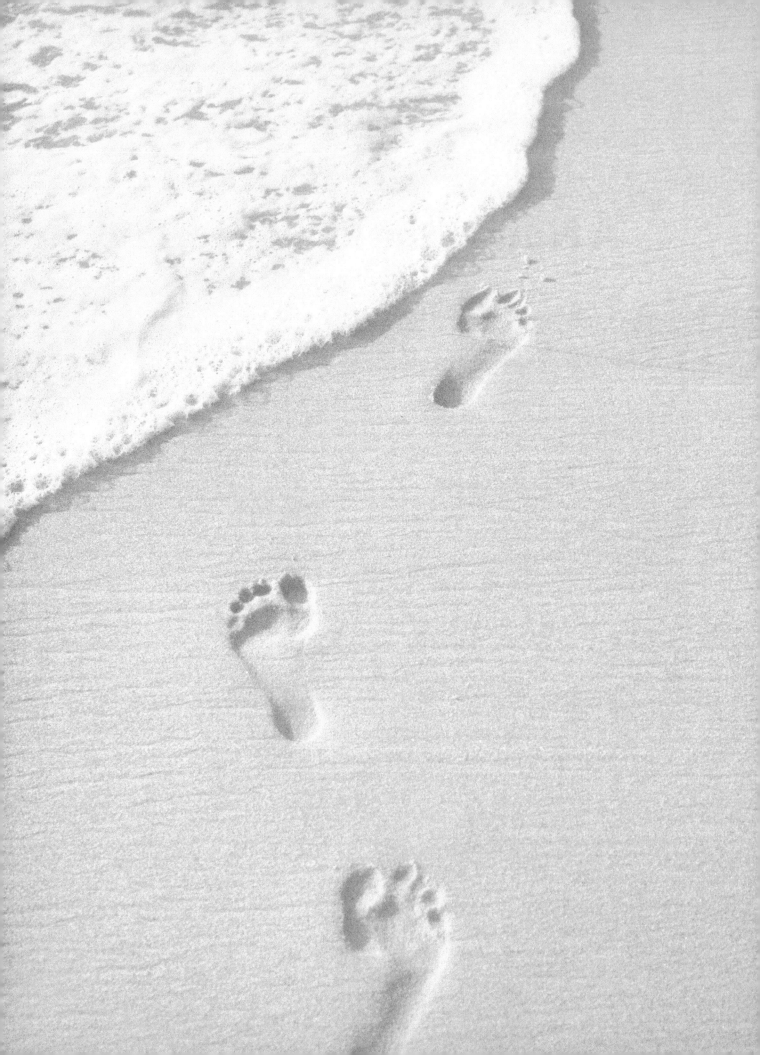

Introduction

The children tumble into the room, full of energy and enthusiasm. They look around, making sure everything is in its place. Yes, the teacher is here. The music is playing and the mats are being laid out in the same careful way that they are every week.

The kids take off their shoes, then rush to play Mat Tag as they wait for the others to arrive. Then, on "Five, four, three, two, one," they are all in their places on their mats, lying on their backs with their hands on their stomachs. Their breaths make their bellies rise up and down—little mountains, rising and falling.

Ah, stillness. After a full day of school, they now have a chance to rest, to turn inward, to listen to the rhythms of their own bodies. Then they roll forward and back a few times, ending up seated in a cross-legged position with their hands together at their hearts. They breathe in, then take their hands up over their heads. As they exhale, they slowly extend their arms out to their sides and back to their hearts. It's like a beautiful dance, how their arms and breath move together. A thoughtful peace falls over the room.

After a few rounds, they shut their eyes and imagine someone they would like to send their heart-thoughts to. As they inhale and bring their arms over their heads, they hold the image of that person in their minds, and as they exhale and their arms go out to their sides, they send that person the thoughts from their hearts. The magic deepens. The movement slows down. Their intention behind their movements is obvious.

After three more breaths, they share. Joe says, "I sent my thoughts to my brother in Iraq."

"I'm sorry," says Heather. "I'll send your brother heart-thoughts next time."

"Me, too," says Juan. "That would be hard. I hope he doesn't get hurt."

Joe nods and says, "Me, too. I send him power every single day because he is very important to me."

Another student, Steven, shares that he has sent his thoughts to his friend Juan, who sits next to him. Juan's big brown eyes widen with surprise. He looks at Steven and then down at the ground as he thanks him. A few moments later, Juan asks if we can do Volcano Breath one more time. We do, and Juan sends his kind thoughts to Steven. Steven looks him in the eye and thanks him.

A few more students share their thoughts and feelings. Then we move into a more physical practice, the students stand at the front end of their mats in Mountain, a simple yoga pose. They feel the strength in their bodies. With their feet anchored to the ground and their heads lifting toward the sky, they imagine themselves as strong as mountains. They close their eyes and think of someone in their lives who they want to be strong for.

"My little sister," says Heather.

"My mom," Steven says.

"My iguana," says Freddie.

"My brother," Joe adds.

Fueled by their intention to be strong for those they love—their parents, siblings, pets, their friends and other family members—we move into a linked series of yoga poses that strengthens and stretches the whole body.

After a few rounds, individual students step to the front mat and lead the others in the flow. They remind each other to stay strong. They compliment one another, listen to one another, and move in unison toward greater physical, emotional, and mental strength.

Next we play Trust Walk and Sensory Adventure, a game designed to develop personal awareness, sensitivity, and trust. The children laugh, surprise each other, and have the chance to be light and playful. They love the opportunity to play with their teacher. Everyone is learning.

Toward the end of class, the students do a few gentle twists and more Belly Breaths to calm their bodies again. Then they lie down for a relaxation process—in this case, a guided story that includes characters and places requested by the students. These are woven into the story to help develop imagination and integrate the children's experiences.

Joe asks to have his brother in the story, while Juan asks for a fire-breathing dragon. Freddie wants his iguana there. As the teacher begins the tale, she tells the children that they will each find a special gift in the story, or meet a friend who has an important note for them. The students lie in rapt attention, each waiting for their image to appear. Afterward, they share their thoughts and feelings.

"My brother was there, and he told me that he missed me," Joe says.

"How did that feel?" the teacher asks.

"Good," he says, and smiles.

When children are given the opportunity to come to stillness and share from their hearts, beautiful things happen. They cultivate their own compassion and sensitivity and begin caring deeply for one another. In our Yoga Calm classes, we are reminded over and over again of the inherent goodness in children. And we become acutely aware of our responsibility as adults to protect, guide, and develop that goodness.

*   *   *

Our Story

The seeds of Yoga Calm were planted in both of us years ago, when we were teens. Jim was 16 when introduced to yoga through his study of the martial arts. An energetic and highly active young man, he found that the practice helped him achieve focus and discipline. At the same age, Lynea discovered yoga at a church camp on the shores of beautiful Lake Tahoe. Having experienced some crucial losses early in life, she found through the practice a place of healing and inner peace.

When we met in a dance class in 1995, we were each excited to have found a partner who shared a love of yoga, and we set out to pursue a practice together. At the time, Jim had just left the business world for a more fulfilling job that blended his lifelong interests in science and the outdoors: directing a National Science Foundation–funded environmental education program for children. Lynea had been working with children of all ages for years, as an educator in a variety of settings and then as a counselor in the public schools. As she continued this work, which she still does today, Jim decided to act on our shared desire to bring yoga to others. He built our studio, Still Moving Yoga, and began teaching full time.

Yoga Calm sprouted early in the new millennium, when Lynea began to see a steady increase of students with extreme behavioral issues. Some had been diagnosed with severe attention deficit hyperactivity disorder (ADHD), while others had been diagnosed with oppositional defiant disorder or autism. Some came from traumatic backgrounds. As their counselor, Lynea observed how hard it was for them to sit in a group and share. She felt they needed opportunities to manage and direct their strong feelings and impulses—like those of the young boy she saw one day crouched under a table in a fetal position, screaming, "Help me! Can anyone please help me!" This child's obvious pain touched her deeply. She wanted to help him find peace in his small body. She could see the trauma he physically held, how his instinct to protect himself drove him under the table—a common way for wounded children to self-soothe.

Through her own yoga practice and counseling work, Lynea had learned to listen to the body and the heart to find a path toward healing. When the body opens, emotions can be released, and the body and heart grow strong together. She wanted to help her students experience these benefits. She believed that a practice that was both physically and emotionally supportive could help these children and others like them.

At home, Lynea would share with Jim her concerns about the children. We would have long talks about how we could use yoga to help them learn the things that have helped us in our individual journeys toward healing and inner peace. Lynea began to incorporate physical yoga activities into her work with the kids, reporting on the effects each evening. Jim, as a self-described ADHD adult, was a good listener and creative in developing games and activities. Occasionally, he'd come out to the school, and together, we'd try out these activities with the kids. The students loved Jim's playful nature, strength, and enthusiasm as he showed them new poses—"yoga tricks," as they called them.

Still, it wasn't easy. In fact, teaching yoga to behavior-disordered children started out as a nightmare. The kids didn't listen. They fought over the mats. They whined that it was too hard. At one point, Lynea wanted to just give up, but thanks to teacher encouragement and support, we kept on. And after a while, we began to see a change in the students. They started to show greater ability to be still. They began to show compassion and support for one another. Some students would come into the classroom to practice yoga during their lunch recess. Something was beginning to shift.

It took time to learn how to effectively and successfully blend the two practices of physical yoga and social/emotional skill-building. Some days, the yoga would stimulate a great deal of emotion, and the children would spend most of their time processing their feelings. Other days, the students wanted only to do physical poses, and little emotion was addressed. Lynea began to trust the group process and found ways to direct the poses to help students maintain a sense of control when emotions emerged. Over time, a sense of community developed in the yoga class. The students gradually became more skilled at directing their own emotion and helping one another through it. Lynea recalls one day when they asked to do a series of poses in complete silence and insisted that this meant that she had to stay quiet, as well. It was a beautiful experience, watching them all move together. They had come a long way.

Challenges Facing Children Today

When we have the privilege of observing the fragile beauty of children's open hearts and minds, we understand how important it is to provide them with a safe and supportive environment, the tools for self-discovery, and the skills they will need to maneuver successfully through life. Unfortunately, not everyone in our culture holds children's lives sacred. As counselors, teachers, and parents, we regularly encounter the negative effects of shattered and chaotic environments. It is painful to sit with a child who has been sexually or physically abused. It is maddening to see and hear about the violent media that adults create and sell, perpetuating a climate of fear and hostility.

Counselors for children are often asked interesting questions: You're doing support groups for kids? Isn't that a little young to start psychoanalyzing them? What kind of issues can a five-year-old child have? The answers silence those who ask such questions: the children have been removed from their home and are in foster care; a parent died in a car accident; a little brother died of sudden infant death syndrome.

Tragedy can come at any age. When it does, it is vital to have a community of support and the skills necessary to move through the pain.

Often overlooked because it seems so commonplace now, divorce is another traumatic source of emotional loss for children. With over half of marriages ending in divorce and the number of single-parent households doubling since 1960, divorce is second only to death as a significant stressor in children's lives. The emotional cost is profound, with children affected by divorce losing, on average, a grade year and a half of academics. And while the federal government spends billions of dollars trying to improve individual math and reading scores, with modest results, up to 30 percent of students are dropping out of high school in what's been painted as a portrait of emotional disengagement.

The disengagement is also a physical one, with the proportion of public school students in daily PE classes declining from 42 percent in 1991 to 33 percent in 2005. This has happened as schools have cut back or eliminated gym to squeeze in more time for core academics and the strict demands of the federal No Child Left Behind Act. This flies in the face of research showing that higher levels of fitness are associated with higher academic achievement, enhanced self-esteem, and reduced feelings of depression and anxiety. The imbalanced focus on academics has left in its wake only modest academic results, as well as obesity rates that, since 1980, have doubled for children and tripled for teens.

Contributing to the health, academic, and emotional stressors facing children today are the rising levels of electronic media consumption—violent media, especially. According to one study, by the age of eighteen, the average teen has spent nearly 16,000 hours in front of the television—compared to just 13,000 hours in the classroom—viewing thousands of violent acts in the process. Sadly, violence is a big part of such media's appeal—and of its insidiousness. Increased time spent on television and video games has been linked to increases in obesity and antisocial behavior, loss of quality sleep and an accompanying increase in health problems, and decrease in reading scores. Meanwhile, with ever more external stimulation, children's imagination languishes.

The Positive Forces and Elements in Children's Lives

It's important to note the positive forces and elements in children's lives that can be tapped into in the course of helping them learn to manage stress. These include greater gender equality and cultural diversity; more open communication about abuse and other formerly taboo issues; greater number of and access to health care alternatives, treatment options and integrated modalities to help children manage physical and emotional needs; the availability of helpful medications to improve the quality of life of those suffering from mental illness; and a greater and ever-increasing number of wonderful, caring people working with children to help them improve their lives.

The Need for Balanced Education

Of course, the focus on academic learning is important, but something is clearly wrong when it comes at the expense of children's emotional and physical well-being. For children to truly thrive, all aspects must be addressed. And when they are, they are mutually supportive. We see this, for instance, in the well-documented benefits of physical activity on fitness, learning, and emotional health. And new research shows what we have intuitively known for years: that the reduction of stress, the development of social/emotional skills, and a sense of well-being have corresponding health and academic benefits. Consider the following:

- A growing body of literature suggests that a deliberate and comprehensive approach to teaching children social and emotional skills can raise their grades and test scores, bolster their enthusiasm for learning, reduce behavior problems, and enhance the brain's cognitive functions.

- Because the emotional centers of the brain are very connected to the thinking and learning centers of the brain, we know that people who are better able to control their emotions and moods are more effective learners.

- Prosocial behaviors exhibited by students in the classroom were found to be better predictors of academic achievement than were their standardized test scores.

- School interventions that increase social and emotional competence result in higher achievement levels, although the reverse is not true (i.e., academic enrichment does not increase social responsibility).

- Studies dating back to the 1960s show that high anxiety cripples test-taking and academic performance.

In challenging times, new opportunities for growth arise. School inclusion, cultural diversity, technology, changing family structures, environmental changes, and the like are driving Western civilization toward a new awareness of our interconnectedness and the importance of holistic solutions. At issue is the need to reduce children's stress while balancing academics with more support and training in physical and emotional health.

Yoga Calm

To address this need for a balanced approach, Yoga Calm melds the traditional Hatha yoga practices of mindfulness, physical poses, and nervous-system regulation with social/emotional skill development and emotional support and guidance. The yoga helps children become more aware of their bodies, learn to treat themselves well, and make healthy life choices. The cognitive skills develop mental strength, positive self-concepts, and imagination. The social/emotional training and guidance allow them to tell their stories, feel and express their emotions, and learn to give and receive support.

Using this kind of integrated approach, we serve the whole child, educators become more effective, and schools become more efficient at addressing competing curriculum demands.

Additionally, Yoga Calm's focus on principles instead of procedures provides opportunities for children with different capabilities to participate together in the same classroom. This simultaneously empowers both students and teachers to creatively respond to what is needed in the present moment. Yoga Calm principles aim to equip children with the skills, self-understanding, and self-confidence they need to thrive in the modern world.

This integrated and principle-based approach also supports the health and wellness of school staff—providing them opportunities to participate in yoga and in stress-reduction and wellness activities. The meaning of the word yoga is "to unite," and Yoga Calm's goal is to support the complete health and wellness of children as well as their teachers, families, and communities.

It is from the support of our community that we have developed the games and activities described in this book to help children find a positive path in life. And as our teachers gave to us, so we give. We recognize the beauty and promise of children, and are committed to drawing out their unique gifts and thus being true to the Latin root of the word "education": *educere*, meaning "to lead out."

Yoga Calm for Children is our gift and an offering of hope and support to children and to those who work to protect and enhance their lives.

> *The reduction of stress, the development of social/emotional skills, and a sense of well-being have corresponding health and academic benefits.*

What Is Yoga? 1
What Is Yoga Calm?

Yoga, Yoga, Yoga!

Yoga seems to be everywhere these days—from celebrity interviews and magazine covers to workplace classes. Even McDonald's—yes, McDonald's!—has offered instructional DVDs with some of its meals. This exploding popularity of yoga in the West is no accident. Its stress-reduction and health-promotion benefits are widely recognized by health care practitioners and laypeople alike as a seemingly perfect antidote to our demanding modern lifestyles.

But beyond a good hamstring stretch and respite from the world, what exactly is yoga? An online search or perusal of your local bookstore will reveal an astonishing array of practices, beliefs, and philosophies. While a bit overwhelming to the novice, this diversity of expression is one of the keys to yoga's longevity and effectiveness. It is a living tradition that has evolved and adapted over thousands of years to meet human needs.

At the heart of this tradition is the desire to be healthy and whole, to integrate the various aspects of our human nature. In fact, the very meaning of the Sanskrit word for yoga is "to yoke or unite." This is commonly translated as the integration or harmonizing of the body, mind, and spirit, and as a comprehensive approach to well-being, yoga typically includes systematic training in five basic areas:

- Breathing—to relax and rejuvenate the body and mind through the development of healthy breathing patterns and techniques that increase energy and release tension

- Exercise—to regulate the nervous system, develop strength, improve circulation, release tension, and increase flexibility through the practice of physical poses

- Meditation and Positive Thinking—to develop focus, gain self-control, and cultivate inner peace

- Lifestyle—to grow aware of the effects of the choices we make and learn to choose wisely, knowing that all we do and experience contributes to our overall health

- Relaxation—to calm the emotions and nervous system, integrate, and give the body a chance to recharge

No one knows exactly when yoga began, but it certainly predates written history. In the Indus Valley, stone carvings dating back 3,500 years or more depict figures in yoga positions. This puts its origins even further back than the beginnings of Hinduism—a fact that puts to rest the common misconception that yoga is rooted in Hinduism. On the contrary, Hinduism's religious structures evolved much later and incorporated some yogic practices. Since then, many other religions and organizations have also incorporated practices and ideas related to yoga. But yoga itself is not a religion.

Yoga probably arrived in the United States in the late 1800s, but it did not become widely known until the 1960s, as part of the youth culture's growing interest in the East. As more became known about the beneficial effects of yoga as a means of stress management and improving health and well-being, the practice gained more acceptance and respect. Since the 1990s, it has absolutely exploded in popularity. Today, approximately 16.5 million Americans are taking classes in Hatha yoga—the branch of yoga that combines physical poses, or *asanas*, with breathing techniques, or *pranayama*. These classes meet in a wide variety of settings including yoga studios, health clubs, businesses, churches, physical therapy clinics, and hospitals.

An estimated 2,000 studies of the health benefits of yoga have been conducted since the 1920s, with much of this research taking place over the past fifteen years. Arguably, it was Dean Ornish's landmark 1983 study that spurred Western medicine's adoption of yoga within the realm of what's commonly called "complementary medicine." The Ornish study showed that yoga training plus dietary changes were associated with a fourteen-point drop in serum cholesterol levels and greater heart efficiency in just three weeks' time. Such studies—and many others that have supported and built upon Ornish's work—have encouraged physicians to recommend yoga practice not just for patients at risk of heart disease, but for those with back pain, arthritis, depression, and other chronic conditions.

Yoga Brought into the Schools

Before the 1990s, most yoga training and practices in the West were adult-oriented, emphasizing physical poses, mental relaxation and meditation techniques, and some breathing techniques. The relatively few children's yoga classes that existed then were typically outside the school environment and focused on simple physical poses and games. But due to a convergence of forces around the turn of the 21st century, this began to change.

As awareness of the health benefits of yoga grew among adults, it was only a matter of time before educators and children's health providers would apply it to the needs of youth. As mentioned above, American schools and families today face daunting challenges: low academic achievement; increasing rates of autism, depression, anxiety, asthma, and obesity; unfunded mandates to increase scores on standardized tests in regular and special education; reductions in state and federal education budgets; loss of physical education, sports, music, dance, and art programs; and big-budget advertising by multinational companies selling high-fat, high-calorie foods. Schools also deal with attention-challenges, violence, and a decline in parent involvement.

These factors, and the mainstreaming of students with various physical and behavioral disabilities into the classroom, have increased the responsibilities of teachers to provide not only academic training, but also special-needs adaptations, physical fitness training, and emotional support services. In some cases, teachers may even function as frontline social workers. The resulting stress for teachers and students alike is taking its toll. According to a 2002 *Washington Post* report, "Even without the pressures of a violent crisis, teachers complain that their jobs, while rewarding, are getting harder because of too few resources, too much paperwork, crowded classrooms, students with emotional problems, low pay and high-stakes standardized tests."

As these forces converged with public awareness of both the physical and mental health benefits of yoga, teachers, administrators, social workers, and psychologists began to apply some of the more common principles and practices of yoga to address the challenges of educating children today. That these efforts have been successful is borne out by numerous research studies from around the globe, including a noteworthy 2007 study from Purdue University. Looking at K-5 student outcomes at six U.S. and Canadian schools that had incorporated the Yoga Kids Tools for Schools program, the research team found significant positive effects on the children's academic achievement, personal attributes, relationships, and general health. Other key recent research is summarized below.

From "School-Based Yoga Supports Academic Achievement and Student Wellness"

by Karma Carpenter, LICSW, RYT

Reprinted by permission

Academic Performance

In 2000, cardiologist Herbert Benson led a research team to study the relationship between exposure to a relaxation-response curriculum and academic achievement among middle school students. Teachers were trained to teach their students relaxation exercises and self-care strategies. Those who had more than two semesters' worth of exposure to the relaxation curriculum earned higher marks in GPA, work habits and cooperation, than students who did not, and maintained this improvement for at least two years.

The Accelerated School (TAS) in South Central Los Angeles is a flagship school which integrates yoga with its teaching. According to co-founder Kevin Sved, "Unless you're fully engaging the minds *and* bodies of the children, they're not going to be as productive" (emphasis added). The results of the TAS approach bear this out. Between 1997 and 2001, TAS saw an amazing 93% increase in Stanford Achievement Test scores. Attendance averages 94%—very high in the LA Unified School District. In May 2001, it was recognized by *Time* magazine as Elementary School of the Year.

Self-Esteem, Discipline, and Physical Fitness

A 2003 study of the YogaEd program at TAS found that yoga class participation not only helped students improve their attitudes toward themselves, but their behavior also improved, as seen in the vastly lower rate of discipline referrals. These students also ranked as more physically fit, with more than 23 percent more TAS students meeting the standards for physical fitness than students at other schools in the district.

Oppositional and ADHD Subscales and Indices

Preliminary findings suggest that yoga is effective as a complementary and alternative method for addressing ADHD and may be especially effective later in the day when medications wear off. Jensen and Kenny recommend larger studies involving yoga programs integrated into school curriculum.

Emotional Balance, Reducing Fears

In a 2003 study of 48 fifth grade students, Stueck and Gloeckner found that yoga training increased emotional balance and reduced fears, feelings of helplessness and aggression. They also found that the participants transferred the learned breathing techniques and self-instructions to situations beyond school.

Stress Reduction and Behavior Support

A 2014 Wayne State University study of the Yoga Calm program at a low-SES Detroit-area elementary school showed a decrease in stress and an improvement in student attention and on-task behavior. Additionally, the study found students' behavior improved both in the classroom and outside of school. Students reported enjoyment of yoga and unprompted use of Yoga Calm techniques to deal with anger, aggression and the need to regulate.

It is reported that today in the United States alone, thousands of teachers have been introduced to school-based yoga and hundreds of schools are implementing programs, with positive, and in some cases, remarkable results. While all programs emphasize the physical and mental integration that is the hallmark of yoga for schools—and most include emotional components—Yoga Calm's approach is unique. With its emphasis on social and emotional skill development, teachers support students in reducing the stress in their lives and managing emotions. Our discussions with educators reveal that teaching stress management and social/emotional skills is a key missing link in today's education system. What's more, addressing these two areas helps support students outside of school, by giving them the strategies and tools they need to deal successfully with the many pressures in their lives.

Children and Stress

We are not born knowing how to deal with stress, especially the psychological kind. Rather, this is a skill we learn, most commonly by observing others. And considering that stress-related illnesses have been America's number one health problem over the past twenty years, it's obvious that we can do better.

But just what are we talking about when we talk about stress?

Most simply, stress is a medical term for a wide range of strong external stimuli, both physiological and psychological, that can cause a physiological response. First described by Hans Selye in the journal *Nature* in 1936, a stressor is anything in the outside world that can knock you off balance, and the sheer variety of stressors in children's lives today has certainly accomplished this. Many of these are listed in the Children's Stress Inventory, reprinted below, which you may find helpful in understanding a child's particular stress situation.

From *The Center For Applied Research in Education, Inc. 1986.*

Check any of the following events that have occurred in the child's life in the past twelve months and add up the total mean values. The total score can be used to predict his/her chance of suffering serious illness within the next two years. For example, a total score that is less than 150 means that the child may have only a 37 percent chance of becoming ill. A score between 150-300 increases the chance of getting sick to 51 percent. A score over 300 increases the odds of getting sick to 80 percent.

LIFE EVENT	MEAN VALUE	LIFE EVENT	MEAN VALUE
1. A parent has died	100	20. Feeling threatened (trouble with a bully or gang)	31
2. Parents have divorced	73	21. Losing or being robbed of a valuable or possession	30
3. Parents have separated	65	22. Major changes in responsibilities at home	29
4. Separation from parents	63	23. Brother or sister leaves home	29
5. Death of a close family member	63	24. Trouble with relatives other than parents or siblings	29
6. Major personal injury or illness	53	25. Outstanding personal achievement and recognition	28
7. Remarriage of a parent (getting a new parent)	50	26. Major changes in living conditions	25
8. A parent was fired or you were expelled from school	47	27. Personal habits change (e.g., style of dress, people you hang out with)	24
9. Parents got back together after separating	45	28. Trouble with a teacher	23
10. Parent stops working to stay at home or returns to work	45	29. Major change in your school schedule or conditions	20
11. Major change in health or behavior of family member	44	30. Change in where you live	20
12. Pregnancy of family member	40	31. Changing to a new school	20
13. Problems in school	39	32. Major change in the usual type or amount of recreation	19
14. Gaining a new famiy member (e.g., birth, adoption, grandparent moves in)	39	33. Major change in religious activities	19
15. Major school change (e.g., class or teacher change, failing subjects)	39	34. Major change in school activities	18
16. Family financial state changes a great deal	38	35. Major change in sleep habits	16
17. Death or serious illness of a close friend	37	36. Major change in family get-togethers	15
18. A new activity begins (one that takes up a lot of time and energy, e.g., dance or music lessons, sports team, computer classes after school)	36	37. Major change in eating habits	15
		38. Vacation	13
19. Major change in the number of arguments with parents or brothers and sisters	35	39. Holidays or birthdays	12
		40. Punished for doing something wrong	11

Physiologist Walter Canon coined the phrase *fight or flight* to describe the basic stress response, emphasizing its positive adaptive aspects in physical survival situations—such as being chased by a wild and hungry animal. Under this kind of acute stress, the human body undergoes a number of key changes. The sympathetic nervous system activates the release of stress hormones and neurotransmitters that prime the heart, lungs, circulation, metabolism, immune system, and skin to deal quickly with the threat. Heart rate and blood pressure increase. Breathing speeds up and the spleen releases red and white blood cells, facilitating greater oxygen intake and transport through the body. Blood is diverted from the skin to support the heart and other muscles, while also reducing the amount of blood that may be lost in the event of injury. Short-term memory, concentration, inhibition, and rational thought are suppressed, as are all nonessential physiological activities (e.g., digestion, cell growth). All this lets you focus completely on the task at hand—repelling or fleeing from the threat. Meanwhile, long-term memory stores the experience for future reference and thus, long-term survival.

Once you're out of harm's way, the parasympathetic nervous system kicks in, reversing the process, allowing the body to rest, recover, and regain energy.

Though most of us will never need to deal with a charging lion, bear, or other wild animal as our distant ancestors regularly did, our fight-or-flight response is just as useful with modern physical threats such as jumping out of the way of a speeding car. Unfortunately, it's not so appropriate for psychological and social stressors. If someone is criticizing you, or you have a big test coming up, you usually can't run or fight. Instead, most of us sit passively while our blood pressure rises, stomach tightens, breathing speeds and grows shallow, and adrenaline surges. When there is no way to act upon or discharge all of that sudden energy, it is the stress response that turns on us.

Though some moderate stress can be positive, if the stress goes on too long the stage is set for physical illness. As Robert Sapolsky shows in his book *Why Zebras Don't Get Ulcers*, although stressors—even massive or chronic ones—don't automatically lead to illness, they do increase the risk of disease. Health risks include compromised immune system function, inhibited growth and even death of brain cells in the hippocampus; osteoporosis; cardiovascular disease; neck, shoulder, and back pain; rheumatoid arthritis; asthma; depression; and diabetes. In children, emotional and physical development may be impaired. And unhealthy ways of reacting to and interacting with the world may become entrenched.

How stress affects an individual depends upon the person's genetic makeup, experience with stress, and how he or she has learned to cope with it. Children under acute or chronic stress may exhibit any of a wide variety of symptoms, many of which are readily observable by parents, teachers, counselors, physicians, and others who regularly interact with children.

These signs of stress, as summarized from *Ready…Set…R.E.L.A.X.* by Jeffrey S. Allen and Roger J. Klein, include:

- Headaches
- Stomach problems, diarrhea, constipation, nausea, heartburn
- Pounding heart
- Aches and pains
- Muscle jerks or tics
- No appetite, constant eating, or a full feeling without having eaten
- Sleeping problems
- Nightmares
- General tiredness
- Shortness of breath
- Dry mouth or throat
- Teeth grinding
- Stuttering
- Uncontrollable crying or inability to cry

- General anxiety or tenseness
- Dizziness and weakness
- Irritability
- Depression
- Propensity to accidents
- General anger
- Feeling overwhelmed, unable to cope, wanting to run away
- Jumpiness, propensity to startle easily
- Boredom
- Always feeling rejected
- Poor concentration
- Never laughing
- Not having friends
- Not finishing homework

" The implications of long-term stress are even greater for children, as emotional and body development can be retarded, and unhealthy ways of inter-reacting with the world become entrenched. "

Obviously, these symptoms of stress should prompt inquiry and possible action to alleviate their causes. If left unattended, they can become impediments to learning, create additional challenges in classroom management, and set the stage for long-term health problems. However, no matter what the source, all children will benefit from learning how to handle their stress in positive, proactive ways—to become *stress-hardy*.

According to Sapolsky, there are a number of behaviors we can rely on to manage stress in our lives—from positive thinking techniques to finding outlets through which to channel frustrations or receive emotional and social support. But the key determinant in successful stress management, he notes—as do other stress researchers—is creating a sense of control. "Change the way even a rat perceives its world," Sapolsky writes, "and you dramatically alter the likelihood of its getting a disease. These ideas are no mere truisms. They are powerful, potentially liberating forces to be harnessed. As a physiologist who has studied stress for many years, I clearly see that the physiology of the system is often no more decisive than the psychology."

Achieving a sense of control, however, can be difficult for children, as so many of their life activities are dictated by others. Thus it's especially important to give them training in what they are able to control—things like how they breathe, what they think, and what they do. These and other stress management recommendations—and how they have informed the development of Yoga Calm—are shown in the graphic below.

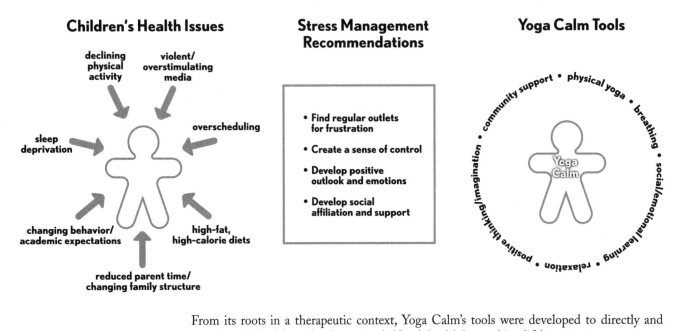

From its roots in a therapeutic context, Yoga Calm's tools were developed to directly and comprehensively address the threats to children's health by teaching lifelong stress management and social/emotional skills. This new approach is effective with a wide range of children, and adults too—further expanding yoga's definition of "union"—and is now playing a catalytic role in the continuing evolution of school-based yoga interventions.

What Makes Yoga Calm Unique?

Yoga Calm is an innovative child education method that integrates fitness, social/emotional, and cognitive learning into five- to forty-minute activities and processes. Its principle-based approach is effective with a broad range of ages, populations, and abilities, and in a wide variety of teaching environments. It includes more than sixty specially designed classroom and therapeutic activities—including yoga-based movement, nervous system regulation techniques, social/emotional skill development, and relaxation and storytelling activities—that provide multiple benefits for educators, parents, and children alike. These benefits include the ability to relax, nurture, and regulate emotions; increased physical fitness, self-confidence, and self-esteem; improved concentration and imagination skills, subject retention, and test scores; enhanced communication, trust, empathy, teamwork, and leadership skills; and the development of healthy life choices.

Yoga Calm's genesis dates to 2002, in the behavior classroom of a rural Oregon elementary school. Since then, schoolteachers, counselors, nurses, and occupational therapists from around the world now use its techniques. Our students have since observed that Yoga Calm helps prepare children for learning and that all types of children are using its skills to handle conflict, identify and express emotions, and manage impulses. Furthermore, these professionals have found that teaching wellness practices like Yoga Calm has reduced their own personal and work-related stress.

Significantly, the program also is adaptable for use in other therapeutic settings, such as children's treatment centers and clinics. One of these is the thirty-year-old Children's Program in Portland, Oregon, which has successfully collaborated with Yoga Calm to provide training for children and teens struggling with ADHD, anxiety, and other mental health concerns.

Over the years, we ourselves have observed amazing results stemming from Yoga Calm practice. We have seen seriously wounded children begin to believe in themselves again. They stand taller, trust their inner instincts, and express their thoughts and emotions with confidence because they have been trained to understand their hearts, minds, and bodies. The ongoing practice has a profound impact on their daily lives.

Integrated Learning

One key reason for its effectiveness and what distinguishes Yoga Calm is its commitment to the balanced development of students' physical, mental, and emotional aspects. Its activities are highly experiential and designed to allow for expression in all three of these areas. It also recognizes that physical, mental, and emotional processes are at work in every activity and values them equally as sources of information and intelligence.

Students and teachers are also encouraged to listen to the needs of each individual, as well as the community, and always respond to the current situation. The program as a whole, in fact, is designed to respond to the present needs of teachers and students, and to take advantage of "teachable moments" that present themselves. It is likewise designed to balance structure and freedom, encouraging students to develop independence and freedom while understanding the interconnectedness of the community and the natural environment. Yoga Calm thus places itself at the center of the three aspects so students can be successful in all areas: physically healthy, academically successful, and emotionally sound.

"Change the way even a rat perceives its world, and you dramatically alter the likelihood of its getting a disease. These ideas... are powerful, potentially liberating forces to be harnessed."

—Robert Sapolsky

This integration of social/emotional development with the physical aspects of yoga makes Yoga Calm unique in the education and yoga communities. And while its mind/body approach is particularly effective when used in therapeutic environments, its techniques can be taught just as effectively by noncounselors.

Research Supporting the Benefits of Integrative Learning

Education, occupational therapy, and mental health literature abounds in examples of the important interrelation of these three dimensions.

Physical Sphere

- Movement and play develop the sensory-motor intelligence that supports intellectual, social, and personal development. (Ayres, 2005)

- Many studies have shown that the greatest yield of nerve growth factors happens when the body engages in complex movement patterns. (Ratey, 2003)

- Over one-third of schoolchildren have a kinesthetic-tactile preference, indicating that movement helps their learning. (Sousa, 1997; Swanson, 1995)

- Higher levels of fitness are associated with higher academic achievement. (California Department of Education, 2002)

- Exercise affects mood, vitality, alertness, and feelings of well-being. (Ratey, 2001)

Social/Emotional Sphere

- Social and emotional skill development—which includes knowing one's feelings, managing emotions, motivating oneself, and empathy and skill in communicating with others—are at the heart of all learning and of primary importance in long-term happiness and health. (Salovey, 1988)

- The emotional centers of the brain are firmly connected to the thinking and learning centers of the brain. People who are better able to control their emotions and moods are more effective learners. (Greenberg, 2004)

- A comprehensive approach to teaching children social and emotional skills can raise grades and test scores, bolster enthusiasm for learning, reduce behavior problems, and enhance the brain's cognitive functions. (*Education Week,* 2003)

- Up to 50 percent of children in schools with social/emotional learning programs show improved achievement scores, and 63 percent of students demonstrate significantly more positive behavior. (Goleman, 2005)

Cognitive Sphere

- Cognition develops self-understanding and awareness of our mental processes and of other's motives, as well as the ability to put these insights to use in conducting one's life and getting along with others. (Gardner, 1989)

- Positive self-statements are important in developing self-confidence and connecting effort and success. (Sousa, 2001)

- A learned positive outlook on life, encompassing hope, trust, self-esteem, and optimism, is a major predictor of subjective well-being. (Lawlor and Fischer, 2006)

What Yoga Calm Looks Like: A Sample Lesson

A Yoga Calm class typically begins with a Stillness activity like Belly Breathing (p. 63). The purpose is to bring the body to stillness and calm the nervous system. After several minutes, the class settles down for Strong Voice (p. 122), a Listening activity in which the children reflect and write on their sources of inner strength. Each child is also asked to think of someone they know who has a strong voice and has taught them to be strong. This engages the mind and the emotions in order to support the physical exercises we are about to practice. Then students engage in a series of yoga poses that provide physical exercise and an energetic release. During the flow of poses they stop and hold themselves in the standing Warrior I pose (p. 98). As the students hold the pose, they are asked to feel their physical strength and listen to their strong voice at the same time.

Next, we move into a social/emotional development activity called Tree Challenge (p. 92): one student stands in Tree (p. 91) while a partner challenges the standing student's strength by making noises, acting goofy, and otherwise trying to be a distraction. One student, Joe, becomes agitated. He yells at his partner and storms off. Several other students ask what's wrong with Joe. Lynea responds, "He's feeling a little frustrated right now. But he's being responsible. He's taking some time away from the group to cool down." Joe looks embarrassed and angry.

At the end of the game, Lynea has the group come into a circle. She says, "Joe's frustration grew big inside him during that activity, and he had trouble managing those feelings. Has anyone else ever had this happen?" The class spends five minutes talking about times when frustration overwhelmed them. We discuss how big emotions can come up when we are being challenged by others, and how these activities help us to grow stronger inside. Joe looks much better now, and the class has had an important lesson in humanity, acceptance, and emotion. The group now closes the session with a yoga Twist (p. 95), more Belly Breathing, and a relaxation story that includes people in our lives who help us through frustrating times.

Note how in this flow of activities, the social/emotional process of Strong Voice is merged with the physical poses, and an integrative relaxation experience. Through this sort of integration, children can have a physical, mental, and emotional experience of what it means to be strong and supported. This is powerful learning. The group sharing process takes it a step further by adding a social dimension as well, helping to develop the children's empathy, compassion, communication skills, and self-empowerment. Finally, the relaxation story develops the imagination and gives the children an opportunity to integrate, recharge, and transition.

Yoga Calm Principles and Tools

When children learn to quiet their minds and bodies and educate themselves about their emotional, physical, and mental health, they become more competent in many areas. They start to understand the underlying causes of conflict and disease, they make better choices, and they learn to navigate through life with greater compassion and skill. Yoga Calm meets these developmental needs by applying five guiding principles. These principles are the themes and goals that underlie all Yoga Calm processes and guide in their implementation.

Principles

Stillness

Stillness is the ability to quiet the mind and body; to be self-aware; to develop sensitivity, self-control, and self-regulation.

Listening

Listening is the ability to tune in to what the heart, mind, and body have to say. This is important for developing self-understanding, discrimination, self-regulation, and imagination. Appropriate listening reduces the chances of injury and self-destructive behavior.

Grounding

Grounding is the ability to connect to the earth, to be physically present in the body, and to develop a sense of competence, physical safety, and security. A strong sense of balance and other healthy sensory-motor functions are building blocks for academic, behavioral, and emotional growth.

Strength

Physical Strength helps prevent injury and disease and develops capability, confidence, and self-esteem based on measurable outcomes. Mental Strength is the use of positive self-talk, respecting boundaries, and monitoring the things taken into the mind and body. Emotional Strength is the ability to feel, identify, and express feelings without harming oneself or others. Emotional Strength is developed in the social/emotional processes and counseling strategies used in Yoga Calm.

Community

Community nurtures the ability to give and receive support, as well as develop compassion, communication skills, and other abilities necessary to live cooperatively with others.

This focus on principles allows Yoga Calm processes to be adapted to many ages, abilities, and environments. For example, in a classroom with students of diverse abilities, Stillness processes can be explored in a chair or while standing; Listening processes can be performed by all; and Community support can be displayed in many ways, such as simply giving attention, encouragement, or respect.

In the second half of this book, you will be introduced to five groups of activities that are used in Yoga Calm to develop these five principles. Here, we introduce the five groups briefly.

Tools

Breath Work slows the nervous system, helps develop self-control, and connects children with their feelings and inner world.

Yoga-Based Activities release physical and emotional energy and help children learn teamwork and develop strength, concentration, and self-confidence, as well as physical and mental flexibility.

Social/Emotional Activities develop skills in identifying feelings, elicit compassion and sensitivity, and help students learn teamwork and communication skills.

Guided Relaxations use storytelling, relaxation, and quieting techniques that calm the body and mind, allowing students to develop their imagination and integrate emotional and cognitive experiences.

Emotional Guidance acknowledges and appropriately responds to emotion as it rises, which is essential in helping children understand and integrate their emotional experiences.

Emotions, of course, are what make us human. They motivate and drive our behavior and underlie our success in the world. Because of this, we'd like to spend a bit more time describing the role of social/emotional skill development in the Yoga Calm curriculum before exploring Yoga Calm principles and activities in detail.

Social/Emotional Training and Emotional Guidance

Teachers and counselors report seeing more and more children coming to school without good training in social and emotional skills. Respect, managing conflict, trustworthiness, honesty—all these and more must be taught. And everyone who encounters children is involved in the teaching: the parent who tells the child to get off the display case; the grocery clerk who thanks the child for being a good helper to his or her parent or guardian; the bus driver who requires children to stay in their seats and show respect; those who create programs in the media that model positive values. Such training is woven through every aspect of life.

For children diagnosed with autism, ADHD, and other behavioral disorders, these social/emotional skills need to be specifically broken down and practiced on an ongoing basis. For children who don't naturally possess the skills, basic strategies such as identifying and expressing feelings—or reading another person's facial expression—must be taught. And all children need opportunities to learn self-esteem, self-care, and effective communication skills.

Yoga Calm provides a full set of social/emotional skill-building activities and games for practice, which are presented in the second half of this book. By combining these with yoga practice and cognitive skill development, the Yoga Calm method helps teachers, counselors, therapists, and parents effectively address children's basic needs of community, safety, structure, discipline, personal health, and self-control. As children gain skills in these areas, they begin to naturally care for themselves and others, and their academic productivity improves. The outcome is a calmer, more productive classroom and support and hope for teachers, counselors, therapists, parents, and—of course and above all—students.

While teaching such skills is a crucial tool, there is another unique tool that follows: Emotional Guidance.

Think about learning the skill of driving a car. First, you only read manuals, watch others drive, and perhaps experiment with accelerating, braking, and steering in a driving simulator. Social/emotional games parallel this part of the learning process, giving students opportunities to practice good social skills. Emotional Guidance corresponds with the moment when you finally get in a car and take the wheel. It is no longer a simulation. Hopefully, the past practice has been sufficient to help the student drive successfully and safely. And just as we wouldn't want a nondriver to sit in the seat next to a student driver, we don't want an adult who does not have practice in understanding and appropriately expressing emotion to be guiding children in this area. This is where Emotional Guidance comes into play, helping us respond to emotion as it arises in ourselves and our students. It requires personal practice and a basic understanding of the emotional system of the body and how it operates.

Specifically, Emotional Guidance is the ability to acknowledge strong emotion when it arises in oneself and others, and the skill to respond appropriately to that emotion. It is important to state from the start that we do not expect teachers to be counselors. However, it is also important that teachers have the basic skills to provide "emotional first aid" when needed in their work with children. Indeed, this is more important than ever as increasing numbers of children are coming to school with unmet emotional needs. Yet teachers receive little or no training in this kind of emotional support work. Many report feeling overwhelmed by their students' needs and unequipped to manage the strong emotions that can erupt in the classroom. The reality is that many schools have no counselors, and even in schools where there is one, that person is not always available to assist a child in need.

It is our goal to assist teachers in this area by providing them with a basic understanding of mind/body psychology and how to apply simple counseling techniques. This is covered in chapter 8. Meanwhile, we offer here a brief outline of how the program may be applied within different professions. While Yoga Calm is not only for professionals who work with children—it can be, and is, pursued and practiced by parents and whole families as well—it is important to recognize that different users of this book will have different needs and approaches. So we now turn to this topic before we explore in depth the five Yoga Calm principles and their correspondent practices.

Applications for Different Professions

In practicing Yoga Calm, it's important to choose activities that are appropriate for the specific setting in which they'll be done. Simply, a Yoga Calm practice in a classroom will look different from one in a private counseling office. And since it is a principle-based approach, Yoga Calm focuses not just on the physical aspects of yoga but on a larger picture of human development. Thus each professional can draw from personal experience when leading sessions.

Teachers and Educational Assistants

Schoolteachers without a strong background in yoga should focus on learning preparedness and stress reduction with Yoga Calm's basic breathing, relaxation, and physical activities. These activities relieve stress and nurture concentration skills. The social/emotional development processes in chapter 6 will be useful for developing a supportive classroom community.

When emotions arise in students, teachers should help find a counselor for them. With the needs of students in the modern world, every school should have a counselor available, but if this is not the case in your school, you will need to help the student with "emotional first aid" via the Emotional Guidance tools described in chapter 8.

And to be more adept at teaching the physical poses, we encourage teachers to develop an ongoing yoga practice with an experienced yoga teacher.

" Knowledge is experience; everything else is just information."

—Albert Einstein

Occupational Therapists

Yoga Calm provides a whole new set of tools to work with sensory and nervous system integration issues. Yoga Calm's physical alignment principles provide fresh perspective in working with midline and breath awareness. Its physical poses provide a strong focus on balance, core awareness, and stability. Yoga Calm's breathing, biofeedback, and cognitive tools help with nervous system regulation. And its emotional skills training addresses the social/emotional issues that often accompany sensory integration dysfunction.

Yoga and Physical Education Teachers

Because yoga and physical education teachers typically have more specific training in anatomy and physiology, they can provide more education and practice in the physical poses of Yoga Calm. These are covered in chapters 5 and 9. Emotions can and will come up in yoga, but unless trained as a counselor—and having permission to act in that role—a yoga teacher should not try to counsel his or her students. However, the teacher should be able to respond appropriately to student emotions in the public context of a class. We recommend that teachers develop basic skills in how to deal with emotions, as presented in chapter 8, and keep handy a list of referrals to professionals who can support students.

Counselors

When people begin practicing yoga, they may encounter their emotions and memories. Just lying down and coming into silence can stir thoughts and feelings within an individual. If this person doesn't process or understand these, the body may become more rigid due to the emotion locked inside. For this reason, the blending of yoga and counseling can have a profound healing impact on individuals.

Yoga Calm originated in therapeutic settings and has perhaps its greatest potential there. The breathing and yoga-based activities presented in chapters 4 and 5 can help children get in touch with their feelings at the beginning of a session rather than toward the end, as is often the case. Students come in full of chatter about video games and friends, and then, just as they begin talking about the family fight at home last night, it's time to stop. Thus, the integration of physical activity with counseling can help make better use of the time, and provides a way for children to release emotional energy.

It is often very difficult for young children to sit and process emotions—particularly for children with behavioral needs. But as children move through an active physical practice, they can release—and with counseling practices, cognitively integrate—feelings that have arisen in a session. Yoga Calm's storytelling and relaxation processes, presented in chapter 7, can also help cognitively integrate the experience of a counseling session and help children feel more grounded and safe as they return to class or to their home lives.

In writing *Yoga Calm for Children*, we have kept in mind the needs and particulars of the various professions. Thus, we have included a broad range of activities with many variations and adaptations for different populations and environments. In addition, this book's final chapter and appendices provide sample curricula and lesson plans that will help you apply Yoga Calm activities to specific situations.

But first we take a more in-depth look at the five Yoga Calm principles and how they guide the development and use of all Yoga Calm activities.

Yoga Calm Principles in Action | 2

Historically, yoga practices have encompassed both physical and mental techniques for calming the nervous system—exactly what today's stress researchers recommend. And while these techniques are an important part of yoga, they were designed to serve even greater purposes in the individual and the community—those of personal discovery, wellness, and self-mastery. These overarching principles or philosophies of yoga invite creativity and flexibility in responding to needs; empower individuals through self-study, exploration, and discernment; and guide without dictating. The cultivation of these yogic attitudes is at the heart of yoga and a key determinant in its effectiveness, adaptability, and longevity.

Stillness

When I first met nine-year-old Barton, he talked nonstop. He explained that he never cried because once when he cried at his last school, even his best friend laughed at him. His dad told him that boys aren't supposed to cry. "But my dad's not the best person to listen to, you see, because he uses drugs, and that's why I live with my mom now." Then he went on and on about his father's drug use and how scary it was to live in his house because when people came over, you didn't know if you should trust them or not.

I could feel the sorrow in him, and the rage, and I promised him that I would never laugh at him if he cried. I told him that lots of boys cry in my room, and I never make fun of them or laugh at them. He said, "Oh, no, I'm not ever going to cry." Even the thought of it stimulated his need to make a show of his masculinity, so he dropped to the floor right there in my classroom and started doing push-ups—all the while continuing to talk through his heavy breathing. He said that he didn't want to be fat, and he wanted to be strong and taller than his father, who was five feet six inches tall, and he found that the push-ups sometimes prevented him from crying.

One day, Barton came into my room dragging a cardboard box and flying so high that he was frightened of himself. He said that his mom was trying some new medication on him and his heart was racing so fast that he was sure he was going to have a heart attack. We tried calling his mother, but she was unavailable. All the while, he kept getting into his cardboard box and rocking back and forth, then getting out and walking quickly around the room, talking a mile a minute.

I asked him how his body felt. He walked around, moving one hand up and down like a fish, and said, "I'm like the waves of the ocean going up and down." Then he made the waves bigger to demonstrate his feelings to me. He continued talking. I glanced at the clock and realized I had a group of students coming in fifteen minutes. I needed to find some way to help Barton before the students arrived.

"Let's try this, Barton," I said. "Why don't you get in the box and try some slow, deep breaths?" He climbed into the box and pulled his knees up to his chin.

"This is really uncomfortable," he said matter-of-factly. "Sometimes you don't have the best ideas, Mrs. Gillen."

I laughed a little and said, "Well, hold on. Let's see if we can make it more comfortable."

We worked together to cut out the end of the box so his torso could be in but his legs could stretch out. Then I put a pillow in the box and placed a blanket over him. Turning off the lights and putting on some soothing music, I asked him to take deep breaths and see if he could calm his body and be as still as possible. I reassured him that I would stay in the room. From underneath the blanket, he continued to talk, but now he began to slow down. "You know, Mrs. Gillen, I think this is starting to work. That music you're playing is good, you see, and I think it's beginning to calm me down."

I lowered my own voice and worked on keeping myself calm. I talked to him in a soothing, deep voice, and within ten minutes, he had found a route into his own stillness, into his ability to self-soothe.

By the time the group of students arrived, Barton was feeling much better. He named his box his "Soothing Chair," and he demonstrated to the children how it worked. These second-graders were, of course, amazed by his invention, which he continued to use throughout that year. Sometimes he even brought friends into the room to try it. He began attending weekly Yoga Calm classes with me. He took his practice very seriously.

The quality of Stillness is important in developing self-control and self-regulation in students. By learning to still themselves, especially in times of chaos and fear, students gain confidence and become more capable of handling conflict and disruption. They begin to create an inner peace that they can draw on at any time. This quality is developed in all the Yoga Calm physical poses and in the relaxation and quieting processes.

Because children are bouncy and talkative, adults often think that an active, energetic class is what they need. But opportunities to practice Stillness are important for children, as well as for the adults in their lives. When children begin to understand that they can have some control over their own bodies and when they learn to self-soothe, they gain personal power. Sometimes a few minutes of Stillness can break their negative perception of themselves.

A student who had been diagnosed with severe ADHD told me his mother was always saying that he was never in control. We played a game in which we strove to keep our bodies completely still for thirty seconds. After a few tries, he was able to do this. I told him, "See, you've already proven that you can have control for thirty seconds. Tomorrow, let's see if you can do it for a whole minute." His green eyes shot me a look of surprise mixed with suspicion.

Two years later, he sits still and can listen to a novel being read aloud. Sometimes he begs me to continue, even after thirty minutes. By practicing just thirty seconds of Stillness that one day, he gained a new perception of himself.

When working with children with attention disorders, we must first believe that they *can* be still. We have to check our own perceptions about them and open our minds to their potential. For when a whole community has decided that a child is bad or incapable, the child believes and acts accordingly. But as with the student described above, you can start with simple things to teach Stillness: going on a vacation in your mind for thirty seconds, counting your pulse for fifteen seconds, holding completely still for ten seconds—taking small steps. We gradually increase the time, and before long, students are able to come to Stillness easily. A new world opens up to them.

Stillness also encourages children's innate ability to connect to the natural world and observe the beauty in life. This is also a part of our yoga practice with children. We don't think of it as a practice only on mats, though. It is a practice of life. When children who have practiced Stillness in Yoga Calm classes go outside, they tune in to nature's rhythms, and their bodies begin to respond to, and embody, the quality of Stillness that exists in parks, trees, and slow-moving creeks.

Pulse Count helps to engender Stillness and Listening.

On a field trip to a local farm, the owner invited our class of behaviorally challenged students to visit her pond. She told the students they could feed the fish, but they had to walk very quietly on the dock or the fish would swim away.

I said to the students, "You know how to do this. We practice being still every day." Then I asked the liveliest student to demonstrate how quietly he could walk onto the dock. He walked out on tiptoe, not making a sound. The others followed in the same way. Then each silently took a handful of fish food from the owner. And when they tossed it to the water, the pond exploded in flashes of silver jumping fish. The students' faces registered surprise and delight, yet they continued to manage their excitement, whispering only. The sun emerged from behind a cloud. A great blue heron flew out of a large pine and flapped over their heads. It was a spectacular moment made possible by their ability to be still.

At the end of the day, after they'd all taken their seats on the bus, the owner of the farm entered to tell the students that they were the most polite group that had ever visited her farm! Two of the students looked behind them to see if she was referring to someone else, obviously unused to such compliments.

The Stillness activities are designed to help counselors, therapists, and teachers guide students toward greater self-control and sensitivity. Once children learn to practice Stillness, they begin to develop inner peace that can help them through difficult times, as well as the ability to focus and prepare to learn.

Listening

To develop a strong sense of self, students need to listen to the messages that come from their hearts, minds, and bodies. Differentiating between true warning systems in the body and fears or memories from the past is an important skill that will help them make positive choices in their lives.

Molly, an only child, lives with her mother. She doesn't know her father, and her mother is a wonderful, loving person but has a difficult time finding and holding a job. So Molly worries about her mother. She feels anxious and hopeless about their life.

One day during class, Molly was lying very still in a relaxation pose. This was excellent. She had come a long way since a few months earlier, when she could not settle down. She would spend her time poking and bothering students next to her. She still had days like that, but her ability to quiet herself was getting stronger. Now I wanted to help her listen to her own wisdom and find strength inside.

As the students lay on their mats, I asked them to see if they could find the "strong voice" inside of them. I asked them to notice whether the voice was loud or soft, high-pitched or deep. Did the voice sound like anyone? If so, who? Then I said, "See if your strong voice has something to tell you," adding that it was important to listen very carefully, that sometimes it takes time to hear your strong voice.

Afterward, I asked the students to share their experiences. Molly timidly raised her hand. She said her strong voice told her that even if her mother never got a good job, someday she would be old enough to find a job herself and create a positive life. That seed of positive thought began to move Molly out of her hopeless feelings and gave her a vision for her future.

When students learn to listen to the voices and messages that come from inside, they may start to make healthier choices. They can identify and discriminate between different feelings, and they can listen to the wisdom of the body. Indeed, with yoga practice and the help of supportive adults, children can learn to find the voice within that helps guide them toward health and happiness.

It's as a teacher attending a Yoga Calm training reported: she believed the yoga practice of her teen years had prevented her from ever becoming a smoker. Having practiced and developed healthy breathing habits, she was very tuned in to her body's responses, and therefore was acutely aware of the change in her breathing the one time she smoked a cigarette. She never wanted to try that again!

When children begin to listen internally, it is not uncommon for them to name God or Jesus as a source of strength. Because this is an individual child's personal experience, it is appropriate for the child to share this in the structure of the class if so inclined. In fact, when children share their personal experiences of God and religion, it gives the class an opportunity to practice acceptance of different paths.

> *One day after we listened to our inner strength while in Warrior I, Mary, a sixth grader, said that she often thought of Jesus while in these poses. It helped her feel strong, she said. This led to discussion among the students. Some shared their feelings about Jesus. Some said they didn't think about Jesus at all. I listened, honoring each child's experience and modeling understanding and acceptance, very careful in such situations not to give my personal opinion or side with any child.*

It's vital to treat religion as you would any discussion and encourage students to be open and express their experience. If children are to learn how to listen internally, it's important to let them speak about *any* of the things they encounter within.

> *Judy, a fifth grader with a difficult family life, was gently helping a younger student. I commented that Judy had a kind heart. "No, I don't," she said. "I'm not kind at all. I'm really evil. I think evil thoughts all the time."*

> *It was true that Judy could be very mean. She often bullied other children and said cruel, hateful things. I wanted to understand her, so I looked into myself and asked how I have felt when angry. I, too, have felt out of control, which let me understand what Judy meant by feeling "evil." Also I knew that she had good reason to be angry. Her father was in jail for performing a violent act, and her mother had a severe learning disability, making it difficult for her to manage the details of life. So Judy, instead of being mothered, often had to play mother to her mother.*

> *The next day, I invited Judy into my room. I explained that I understood what she had meant and helped her identify her feelings as anger. I told her that sometimes I, too, felt evil when I was angry. I said, "Your angry feelings are not 'you.' They are just feelings. I am going to help you express your anger in ways that won't get you into trouble." Then we went outside and threw a ball against the wall and growled REALLY LOUD!*

> *I continued to work with Judy on her feelings of anger and gave her strategies for expressing her anger. Meanwhile, I had established a group of adults at the school who would take time during the day to notice Judy's kindness and compliment her when they saw her doing good things. And over time, Judy began to make amazing changes. She was brighter and more optimistic. Others liked her more. She laughed and participated more fully in activities. She still had to work on her bullying behavior and was still easily triggered by other students, but she began to change her image of herself. This started because she had the courage to speak honestly about the things she felt when she looked inside and listened.*

When children begin speaking about their thoughts and feelings, they need adults in their lives who are strong enough to listen and understand the things they reveal. If a teacher or counselor has not done the hard work of listening to his or her own sorrows and anger, it will be difficult to stay present with these feelings in a student. An adult who is uncomfortable or impatient with a child's expression may unintentionally communicate this. When there is not time to listen to the student, and the adult feels impatient, it is important for the adult to acknowledge that and either arrange a time to be available or help the student identify someone who can listen (e.g., grandma or grandpa). For when students express strong feelings, it is a dual listening process. The children are tuning in to their feelings, and the adult must tune in to his or her own feelings. This is one way the adult can positively model behaviors that children need to learn.

Indeed, modeling is crucial in teaching the principle of Listening—a point we will return to later.

Grounding

> *Fourth-grader Jessica has been diagnosed with severe ADHD. She is emotional and has a difficult time at recess. She tends to blurt things out, and she lacks good social skills. The children often tease her, and this drives her to tears, which embarrasses her.*

One day in yoga, she asked what she could do when her peers teased her. We practiced standing strong in Mountain (p. 79) with our feet anchored to the earth. We each thought of someone in our life who believes in us and supports us, and we imagined that person holding our feet to the earth. Then we breathed into our bellies and in strong, deep voices said "Stop!" We practiced looking each other in the eye and setting boundaries without yelling or humiliating ourselves. I encouraged Jessica to try these skills on the playground.

Several days later Jessica came bursting into my room full of excitement. "It worked, Mrs. Gillen! It really worked!"

"What worked?" I asked.

"That thing we did in yoga. I pretended I was strong and that my mom was holding onto my feet. I breathed into my belly and told the kids to stop in a deep voice, and guess what! They stopped!"

She looked as though she still didn't quite believe it.

What Jessica had experienced was the ability to ground herself both physically and emotionally. By teaching children to do this, we help them connect to the earth and feel safe and secure, gaining a sense of control over their environment. By bringing their awareness into both the present moment and their physical bodies through activities like those described above, students begin to learn that they can call on their bodies, the earth, and the people in their lives to support them. The ground is always there.

Many children who have been traumatized dissociate from their bodies and have a hard time being present in the physical world. The fast pace of the modern world aggravates this problem. Children's lives are full of many demands and distractions, and many of them spend a majority of their time stimulated by television, video games, cell phones, computers, and other electronic gadgets. They may live in a fantasy world that is not connected to the physical world. They need to develop a sense of physical awareness and safety in their bodies, and to develop a realistic understanding of their abilities and needs.

Balance poses develop Grounding and Strength.

For children to develop good habits for self-care, they need the experience of feeling healthy physically, emotionally, and mentally. When people are perpetually unaware of their bodies, they may believe that a lifestyle involving junk food, video games, and lack of exercise meets their needs. One student informed us that he "relaxed" when he played violent video games. When he learned to check his pulse and understand what relaxation really feels like, he began to see that his body did not, in fact, relax while he was playing these games.

When introducing yoga to students, we start slowly. When poses are taught quickly, without time to develop inner awareness, injuries are more likely to occur, and children can develop a practice that is disconnected from their physical awareness—in essence, creating yet another distraction. We want children to practice and to listen to physical cues at the same time.

Grounding activities help children come into their bodies and prepare them for learning.

Strength

Strength involves not only muscle power—Physical Strength—but also Mental Strength and Emotional Strength. All three are complementary and may be nurtured simultaneously.

Physical Strength

The yoga poses, of course, develop Physical Strength. And as the body becomes physically stronger, students' sense of self is likewise strengthened. They feel safer and less vulnerable. They become more able to participate in physical tasks and the world around them.

In Yoga Calm, we develop Physical Strength by challenging the body in a reasonable manner. We encourage children to push themselves, but also to listen to their physical limitations, and tune in to ensuing emotions and mental processes. As a result, the body begins to grow stronger with encouragement and support—not by being forced into compliance. In this way, Physical Strength grows organically with emotional and cognitive awareness.

Mental Strength

Athletes, successful business executives, and individuals in many professions know the importance of positive self-talk and visualizing positive outcomes. Similarly, by using positive self-talk while in the poses, children practicing Yoga Calm can develop Mental Strength. The guided relaxations further support this, giving students practice in focusing their thoughts and using positive images to help them move toward greater health and success. And as students develop a stronger sense of themselves and their own images and ideas, they are less persuaded by negative external images and behaviors.

Strengthening poses with Listening and positive self-talk help develop Physical, Mental, and Emotional Strength.

Georgia, a sixth-grade student, has been diagnosed with bipolar disorder. Highly sensitive, she has a difficult time at recess because she is often targeted by other students who find it entertaining to set her off.

I found Georgia standing in a balance pose in my office one day, looking at the words posted in bold letters on a bulletin board: "I am strong. I am in control. I can do it. I can be responsible." When I inquired what she was doing, she explained that she'd had some trouble at recess and was using the words and yoga to get herself back in control.

She stood in the balance pose for a few minutes before heading back out to recess. Walking out the door, she called to me, "Thanks, Mrs. Gillen. I use those words all the time!"

Knowing some mental phrases such as the ones Georgia used can help children through difficult times. Positive self-talk trains children to focus their minds on their abilities. It helps keep them from being overwhelmed by fear and insecurities. The words provide a tool to use in moments of fear, anger, or worry. Many children report using these words regularly—in PE, at the doctor's office, during tests, when anxious, and at other times.

Emotional Strength

The process of developing Physical and Mental Strength also supports the development of Emotional Strength. With improved physical and mental control, students can develop the courage to express their emotions and the discipline to process the feelings that arise. Teacher and peer modeling of healthy emotional expression is also essential in developing this quality in students.

Jeremy had problems with extreme work avoidance. Whenever he began something he perceived as difficult, he would lock up and refuse to do anything. This exasperated his parents and teachers. Sometimes it would be impossible to get him back on track when he shut down, and no amount of coercion, threats, or consequences had any impact.

When he began coming to yoga, it was apparent that he was frightened of doing the wrong thing and being criticized. His fear of failure was so great that he would stop before he reached a place where he might fail. So I moved him into practice very slowly. When he was unable to participate, I allowed him to lie on his mat and watch the class. He would come in and out of the poses as he felt ready. To help him through his blocks, I gave him the language to say to himself, "I am strong! I am in control! I can do it!" He made good progress.

Once when the class was doing some very active poses, Jeremy looked extremely frustrated and angry. At one point, he sat down on his mat with a defeated look. I said, "Don't give up, Jeremy. Don't give in to that voice inside your head that wants you to quit."

He looked at me very sternly and said, "I'm not giving up, Mrs. Gillen. I'm sitting down to get my anger under control. I'm trying to tell myself those words you taught me."

"Okay. Good," I said, and we continued with the poses.

Jeremy sat for a few minutes, then got up and joined us in the practice. His yoga was strong and confident! He had really broken through something. I complimented him on how strong he looked.

After class, he told me that he had started to think about his brother, who was in a different foster care situation than he himself was. He said that people had told him he might never see his brother again, and that made him angry. "Then," he said, "I sat down and told myself that it doesn't matter what anyone else said. I will always love my brother,

*and someday I will find a way to see him again." He told me he remembered the last time
he had seen him. He remembered the look in his brother's eyes. He could tell that his brother
loved him.*

This story demonstrates how children begin to use their Physical, Mental, and Emotional
Strength in complementary ways. Instead of running from his feelings of anger or acting out,
Jeremy sat down and listened to them. Then he used the tools he had been taught to remind
himself to think in an empowering way. Once he was able to manage his thoughts around his
feelings about his brother, he took this strength into his body and channeled it into his physical
practice. The results of his developing Mental and Emotional Strength were apparent in his
attitude and composure while doing the poses. And as his competence and discipline in yoga
grew, he increased his ability to move through his work avoidance issues.

Community

The Yoga Calm principle of Community is taught through games and activities that
demonstrate the ways in which communities both support and challenge us.

The development of community support skills such as compassion and caring for one another
begins with helping students learn to express their emotions. Given opportunities to become
aware of both their feelings and the hardships of others, children gain insight into their own and
others' behavior. They begin to want to help others and to see and value themselves as kind and
helpful. Feelings of victimization are reduced, especially among underprivileged populations,
while camaraderie with classmates is actively nurtured. Through all such experiences, students
gain insight into the universal struggles of humanity and begin to understand the value of
community support at a deep level.

> *Charlie, whose mother had recently died in a tragic accident, was a new student in
> Yoga Calm class. After the warm-ups, sixth-grader Jared asked if he could lead a sequence
> of poses. He seemed to have something in mind, so I allowed him to come to the front.
> Before he began the practice he turned to Charlie, looked him right in the eye, and said,
> "I'm doing this yoga for your mother."*
>
> *The whole group grew silent in that moment of honoring. Their yoga was beautiful
> that day.*

Of course, communities can be challenging, too. And these challenges can likewise be utilized
in positive ways. In our social/emotional activities, for instance, we encourage lively conversations
with differing points of view and include games that provide opportunities to challenge and test
one another. We discuss how challenges make us stronger emotionally, physically, and mentally.
Students understand that a game of chess or checkers is more interesting if your opponent
knows how to play and provides some competition. And they recognize that a race is more
interesting if a friend is skilled and provides an incentive to improve.

*Community activities
provide opportunities
to practice social and
emotional skills.*

In fact, we need our families, neighbors, and friends to see our potential and call on us to
do better—and to give feedback and sometimes even criticism. But at times, criticism and
challenging behavior need to be screened out. For example, the playground can be a harsh
environment, particularly for students who have social or emotional issues. Teachers often coach
students to ignore name calling or other bullying behavior, but this is difficult to do. Therefore,
Yoga Calm's community games also provide opportunities to practice effective responses to
bullying and similar negative behavior.

By gaining understanding and skill in dealing with the positives and negatives of community
life, students develop a realistic and healthy model of living.

*   *   *

Through the teaching of these five principles, Yoga Calm helps to provide a safe and
supportive setting and empower lifelong wellness habits for students and teachers alike. It is in
this environment that our greatest potential can be realized.

Setting the Stage for Learning | 3

We now turn to the actual teaching of Yoga Calm. As we have suggested, it begins with an understanding of Yoga Calm principles and how to teach from your yoga and life experiences. Class actually starts before you teach, with the intention you create. But in immediately practical terms, it begins with your preparation of the room.

Creating a Therapeutic Environment

The language of an environment is powerful. Just as one would prepare for important house guests, creating a nice space honors the students and signifies a shift into a new activity.

We recommend you create a routine for the practice. When setting up the space for yoga, it is important to minimize distractions and stimuli. Declutter the room as much as possible and turn off any phones. It helps to draw the shades and turn down the lights. You can place a sign on the door to let others know not to disturb the group while it is in session.

Whatever your preferred routine for your practice, we recommend that you include music. Among music's many proven benefits are its ability to motivate and create enjoyment; to create external auditory cues that favorably affect coordinated movement and proprioceptive control; and to improve behavior and academic performance of children who have emotional and behavioral difficulties. Any music you use should be soft, ambient, slow in tempo, and in long cycles.

To teach relaxation and concentration, we must be "there" first. Use the five minutes before your Yoga Calm session to center yourself. Then, before the students arrive, take the "seat of the teacher." You are the guardian of the space.

Room Preparation Checklist

- Class starts before you teach, with the intention you create.
- Create a routine for the practice.
- Declutter room as much as possible.
- Minimize distractions and stimuli.
- Turn phones off.
- Draw shades.
- Turn down lights.
- Place a sign on the door.
- Turn on music.

This routine of creating a supportive space will pay off in the long run. From both the environment and your attitude, students will recognize that it is time to settle down. Creating a soothing environment provides you with a relaxation break, as well!

Lastly, post the following or similar ground rules visibly in the classroom. Students will use them and look to them when they are reminding other students or introducing yoga to someone new. They also will look at the positive self-talk included in the rules and recite it to themselves when they are doing challenging poses.

Yoga Calm Ground Rules

1. Treat yourself like a king or queen.

2. Respect each other's space.

3. No shoes on the mats (if you use yoga mats).

4. When you are having a difficult time, use positive self-talk: "I am strong. I am in control. I can do it. I can be responsible."

5. If you are struggling, instead of saying "I can't," say "I am not ready for that," or "I have not learned that yet."

Whatever ground rules you choose for your group, aim to keep them simple, visible, and clear.

Classroom Management

It is important to start a yoga class with firm rules and the expectation that children can come into Stillness—the first Yoga Calm principle. If you use mats, make sure they are all the same type and color; this will reduce fighting over who gets which mat. Start with activities that require students to be still, such as Mountain (p. 79) and Pulse Count (p. 83). If the children are having a difficult time, challenge them to be completely still without moving a muscle for thirty seconds. If they move, start again until they are able to stay relatively still for at least fifteen seconds. Additionally, we recommend following the same Yoga Calm routine each time, at least initially, to give students a sense of familiarity, stability, and safety. This will reduce classroom management issues in the long run.

In general and overall, start slowly and easily. Allow your students time to get to know the routine. Then, as they show their readiness—or when you need to vary the routine for interest—gradually add more energetic and challenging poses.

Rewards can be used occasionally when the class starts, but it is best to then phase them out. In treatment centers or behavioral classrooms where a rating system is used, it is helpful to have an aide who can use the system already in place to help manage the class. When a guest instructor goes into a new setting to teach, it is important to acknowledge the system in place and encourage the teachers to share information about the students. The expertise of teachers and aides who work with the children for several hours daily is crucial to a new teacher's success. It is important to work collaboratively.

Beyond rewards, you can encourage positive behaviors by letting students take turns leading poses. This adds interest and gives the students opportunities to lead and be guided by others. However, when they do take turns, be sure that you provide the words so the students aren't giving verbal directions to the class. Rather, they are only to model the movements. And when you lead, focus on those movements you have personally practiced and feel comfortable doing. Avoid poses that you aren't comfortable demonstrating.

Develop a consistent way of asking students to return to their mats. We use a countdown from five to one, which works well, but many teachers find their own routines. The most important thing is to stay consistent, speaking to the children in a firm but loving voice—something it may take practice to do!

Lastly, be patient with yourself and your students. Things will not always go smoothly. Sometimes, students will act out. When they do, it's important to address the situation in the moment and directly. This could be by doing something as simple as having all students sit on their mats and going over the Ground Rules. If the students are tired and unwilling to cooperate, you may want to switch gears and give them a gentle, relaxing class. Some days, we have given thirty-minute relaxation/storytelling sessions when the children needed it.

Here are some additional tips for managing your class when students begin to act out:

Tips for Class Management when Students Act Out

- Inform a student who is acting out that he or she will be leading next, so "you need to get ready."

- Return to Belly Breathing with the Hoberman Sphere (p. 63).

- If some children are unable or unwilling to participate in a particular pose, they can sit on their mats and watch. This is a responsible choice.

- Stop the group and directly address the problem behavior, allowing the students to participate in the conversation.

- Don't proceed to the next activity until the class is still.

- Hold a balance or strengthening pose that requires physical work, timing the students for fifteen seconds to two minutes, depending on the age group and ability.

- Lead them through several Arm Swings (p. 60) as they quietly say to themselves, "I am strong. I am in control. I can do it. I can be responsible."

- If coteaching, have one instructor address the issue while the other continues to teach the class.

Belly Breathing with the Hoberman Sphere.

Teaching from the Body

As I observed a teacher leading a Yoga Calm social skills game in her classroom, I saw that she was losing the class, even though she was leading the activity in an orderly and professional manner. The students were disruptive and interrupting the teacher. There was a Hoberman Sphere on the table behind her and the students cued her to use it. "The ball is behind you," one of the students said. "You should use it." She ignored the suggestion and continued with the lesson.

Watching her, I could see that she was not teaching from her body. Her voice was high, she was talking fast, and she was speaking from her head. It was clear that she was nervous, and the students could feel her anxiety. They were trying to help her out by encouraging her to use the breathing sphere. They knew that she needed to slow herself and the class down. She ignored the cues from the students and was unable to complete the lesson.

Our students are feedback systems. When children act out, adults sometimes blame the children instead of looking at the whole situation. Children often tell us loud and clear what they need, but we may not listen. Good classroom management requires watching the students and responding to their needs without giving up the position of leadership. This is a skill that is learned from experience. Taking the seat of the teacher means to be responsible—or, to put it another way, to respond appropriately to student needs.

Children and adults alike cue off each other's body language. If a parent is anxious, the child feels it and may interpret it to mean that he or she is doing something wrong. The child may try to fix the situation, or get away from it. As a teacher, it is crucial to develop a calm, grounded presence and to teach from this place. Developing your own yoga practice will help.

In the time you give yourself to center and prepare for your students, you may find it useful to use a minute or two to practice a grounding pose. When you speak with your students, speak from your belly and slowly. Repeat again slowly after a few minutes if students aren't listening. Similarly, slow your breath while speaking, anchor your feet, and let your words have weight. Monitor your own nervousness. When you find you are speeding up or speaking from your chest or head, slow yourself down. You may even want to tune in to the breath pattern of one of the students (a calm one!) and speak at the pace of their breath. Also, you can start the class with a breathing exercise and practice it along with the students.

As mentioned above, it's important to be in tune with yourself—to become aware of where and how you are. It pays to be conscious of your own personal issues and to work on them so they don't interfere with your ability to be present. And if you're having a bad day and it's affecting your teaching, be honest and say so. Your students know it anyway.

The Power of Love

> *Preparing for yoga in my classroom, I was in a peaceful mood, and I wanted to share this peace with the students. I turned off the lights, laid out their mats, turned on music, and sprayed lavender scent in the room. I placed a fall leaf on each student's mat as a natural gift for the day. When the students walked in, they could immediately experience the environment I had created for them. As they took off their shoes and came to their mats, one of the students said, "You love us, don't you, Mrs. Gillen?"*

> *It was a bold question. The students stopped and looked at me. It felt as though they had all stopped breathing.*

> *"Yes, I do." I responded.*

> *They all resumed breathing and we moved into class.*

Love is a powerful teaching tool. Every teacher knows the gratification and the reward of helping others. This is what keeps us in a helping profession. Learning to use love without giving oneself away is an ongoing process. When we began working with children, we were ready for the hardships. But what surprised us was the amount of love offered back to us by the students. We have had to learn to be strong enough to receive this love and to use it responsibly.

Through the years, one of the most important things we have learned in this regard is the need to tell students often that you care about them. Be specific:

- I care about your body, your mind, and your heart, and I want to encourage you to treat yourselves like kings and queens.

- I care deeply about your minds, and I want to provide stories and images that will help you be safe and successful.

- I care about your emotions, and I demonstrate this by listening to and understanding the things you tell me. And I expect that you will also show your care for others by showing the same respect.

Similarly, seek to see the individual gifts of each student. Compliment students. Every person needs to be seen and acknowledged for who they are and the gifts they carry. Aim to focus on the positive. Overcorrecting a student, for instance, creates a feeling of defeat. Look for the positive in students and compliment them on their successes.

The Compliment Game (p. 112) gives additional opportunities to practice giving and receiving compliments.

Another way of showing that you care is to provide small natural gifts to students—a little stone, a fresh flower from the garden, their name printed in beautiful lettering. Likewise, you show your care through the practice of sharing with them your honest and authentic self—though only sharing personal information appropriately, of course.

The greatest gift of all, though, is one of the simplest: your bringing your presence to the class.

Practice Patience with Yourself

Becoming a good teacher takes a great deal of time and patience, and making mistakes is an integral part of the learning process. We have days when we try new things that don't work—and days when activities don't work at all, even though we've done them many times successfully. When we teach, we bring ourselves and our students to the edge—the edge of our physical, emotional, and mental limitations. We raise the expectations of students. We test our ability to teach.

The edge of our capabilities is where change occurs—and where mistakes happen. Think of the first time you rode a bike, played baseball, or learned any new skill. You made lots of mistakes! But each time you tried, you got a little better. On the other hand, if the person who taught you expected too much, too fast, you may have given up.

Sometimes the mistakes turn into a new process that amazes everyone.

When making mistakes, it is important to be honest and lighthearted with your students. Covering up a mistake builds distrust in the group. As teachers, we are modeling behavior. If we beat ourselves up when things don't go well, we teach our students to beat themselves up. If we can acknowledge that something didn't go well and then move on, we demonstrate compassion and flexibility.

A lesson in this came from one of our yoga teachers. In a class we were attending, he inadvertently made a remark to a student that hurt her. The student spoke to him about the comment during a break, and at the start of the next session he apologized to her in front of the whole group—over 250 people! It was comforting to see him acknowledge what had happened to the group, and it modeled how graciously a mistake can be cleared up in a class. It also helped us remember that even teachers who have been working for years make mistakes.

This incident reminded us to practice patience and compassion with ourselves.

Yoga Calm Tools
Breath Work | 4

One day, I was having such a difficult time with a children's yoga group that I left the class in utter frustration. Later, one of the students handed me this note: "Dear Mrs. Gillen, I'm very, very sorry for how we acted. Next time I hope we're better. I will try my best to help you keep everyone quiet. I bet when you were in the hall, you were breathing just like you told us to do."

Because breathing patterns have such a profound effect on our general health and mental states, breath awareness is at the heart of almost all yoga practices. Breathing interacts with and affects the cardiovascular, neurological, gastrointestinal, and muscular systems. It also has general effects on sleep patterns, memory, energy levels, and concentration.

Respiration is primarily regulated by involuntary controls through the autonomic branch of the central nervous system so that we breathe automatically, day and night. We don't have to think about breathing—it just happens.

What is not well known is that habitual patterns of breathing can, in turn, affect the autonomic nervous system and have a significant impact on our health. For example, constant stress, disease, poor diet, and parental imprinting can lead to unhealthy breathing habits like breathing too fast. This, in turn, can activate the fight-or-flight response, resulting in anxiety and chronic overstimulation of the sympathetic nervous system. By contrast, relaxing one's muscles and slowing one's breathing can calm the nervous system, lower the heart rate and blood pressure, and turn on the immune system.

Watch a baby at rest and you'll see a good example of healthy breathing. The pattern is relaxed, slow, and wavelike, with every bone, muscle, and organ moving with each breath. Unhealthy breathing, by contrast, is rigid or inappropriate to the situation and often exhibits an excess of muscle tension. While abnormal breathing patterns vary, they are often high in the chest, overly fast, and shallow. Often, there is no pause at the end of the exhalation, or there may be breath holding or gulping. Such habits reinforce feelings of tension, agitation, and anxiousness. By contrast, a healthy breathing pattern elicits a relaxation response, shifting the nervous system from fight-or-flight mode to a state of relaxed alertness.

Yogic traditions have studied and taught the importance of healthy breathing for thousands of years. They teach what modern medical researchers have confirmed is involved in recovering a more natural, healthy breath. The next time you are stressed, try these five steps, particularly focusing on the last two:

1. Become aware of your breathing pattern.

2. Breathe through your nose.

3. Relax. Make sure the abdominal muscles are not overly tense, which can impede the action of our primary breathing muscle, the diaphragm.

4. Slow the breath cycle, particularly the exhalation.

5. Pause at the end of each inhalation and exhalation.

This easy-to-learn technique can be used in any situation where you need to instantly increase your state of relaxation, alertness, or mental clarity.

Healthy Breathing Principles

Awareness

Using hands to practice "belly breathing"

The first step toward recovering and encouraging our natural breath is to become more aware of our breath. While breathing is a natural and automatic process, unhealthy breathing habits are usually unconscious and inappropriate for the situation, such as breathing fast and high in the chest with lots of muscular action while a person is in an inactive state. Such breathing patterns are often imprinted onto children by parental and cultural modeling (think of the "belly in, chest out" look in advertising and at the gym). Often supported by binding clothes and excessive abdominal tension, chest breathing results in less efficient breathing, which in turn stimulates higher respiratory and heart rates.

Unhealthy breathing patterns also can be habituated from long periods of chronic stress. Some researchers have suggested that chronic mouth and chest breathing activates stress receptors in the upper lobes of the lungs, stimulating a sustained fight-or-flight form of arousal, common in states of anxiety and fear.

Our first step in recovering a natural, healthy breath, then, is to develop awareness of our current breathing. Then, with practice of the following simple techniques, we can unlearn bad habits and rediscover our natural breath.

Breathe through Your Nose

Of all the yoga techniques we have taught to our students, nose breathing has been the most profound. As an asthmatic, Jim has significantly relieved his symptoms by adhering strongly to nose breathing.

From our personal experience, and studies of breath physiology, we know that nose breathing is so important because, first, taking air through the nostrils warms, moisturizes, and prepares it for the lungs. Mucous membranes in the nose work together with hairlike cilia to clean and filter our air and ward off infection. The slight resistance provided by nasal breathing provides benefits similar to pursed-lip breathing—a technique often taught to asthmatics to keep the airway open longer, decrease the work of breathing, prolong the exhalation, and slow the breathing rate.

Relax for Diaphragm Efficiency

The diaphragm is our primary breathing mechanism. It is a dome-shaped sheet of muscle and tendon that attaches to the bottom of our rib cage. During inhalation, the diaphragm contracts and flattens downward while the lower rib cage expands. The ensuing vacuum literally pulls air into the lungs. Depending on the body's need for air, chest muscles, such as the intercostals, can also assist in the inhalation by expanding the rib cage. Upon exhalation, the diaphragm, lungs, and chest muscles naturally recoil and, with some help from the abdominal muscles, expel the air.

To make space for the diaphragm's downward descent during inhalation, the abdominal organs have to move down and outward, giving the impression that one is breathing into the belly. If the abdominal muscles are held in too tightly, the diaphragm's action is inhibited, and the resulting loss of efficiency will necessitate using more of the chest muscles to aid in breathing. Therefore many breathing practices start with the recommendation to relax the abdominal muscles and imagine "breathing into your belly." While not technically accurate, and a bit contrived at first, relaxing the abdomen and "breathing into the belly" is an effective tool in reestablishing a more efficient and healthier breath.

Watching an efficient diaphragmatic breath is like watching the waves at the beach, with each breath swelling up from abdomen to chest and back down again.

The chest muscles that expand and lift the rib cage are designed to participate in a secondary and supporting role to the diaphragm. Only during times of high aerobic need should these muscles exert a more dominant role. Because these muscles are less efficient than the diaphragm for breathing, when chest muscles dominate, both breathing and heart rate must increase, which stimulates the sympathetic nervous system—the one responsible for the fight-or-flight response.

> A number of studies have shown a correlation between upper-chest breathing and heart disease. In one study, patients practicing diaphragmatic breathing significantly reduced their chance of a heart attack (Van Dixhoorn, J., 1990). This may be related to how healthy diaphragm function assists with the flow of blood to the heart.

This stimulation of the sympathetic nervous system can start a feedback loop that encourages even more chest breathing, keeping us in a continual state of stress. Thus, chest breathing can be both stress-induced and stress-inducing. This insidious feedback loop can be seen with asthmatics, who typically breathe primarily through their mouths and with overuse of the upper chest muscles.

Experiment for a moment by breathing through your mouth and primarily using your chest muscles. Notice the sensations, feelings, and emotions that accompany this kind of breath. Notice especially the effect on your heart rate. Now, relax, close your mouth, and breathe through your nose. Allow your belly to rise and fall with the breath. Notice the difference.

You have just discovered how relaxed nose breathing facilitates efficient diaphragmatic breathing, which in turn elicits a relaxation response and the calming of the nervous system. Once started, the relaxation response has its own feedback loop, lowering respiration and heart rates, which calms us even more.

Slow the Breath

By consciously slowing our breath, especially the exhalation, we can facilitate the relaxation response even more and can develop some control over how our nervous system responds to our environment. Since the sympathetic and parasympathetic nervous systems are stimulated by inhalation and exhalation, respectively, a relaxed lengthening of the exhalation is especially effective in reducing the heart rate.

In 2002, the Food and Drug Administration acknowledged the effectiveness of breath control for reducing high blood pressure with its approval of RESPeRATE. This device monitors breathing rate and audibly prompts the user to slow down breathing by prolonging exhalation. It has been effective in reducing blood pressure by up to 36/20 (systolic/diastolic) points.

The natural cardio-acceleration during inspiration and cardio-deceleration during expiration is called respiratory sinus arrhythmia and can be experienced in the Pulse Count activity (p. 83) by noting the difference in pulse rates between the inhalation and exhalation phases. Do note, though, that children's resting and maximum heart rates are normally higher than adults'. The Pulse Count activity provides additional information on this point.

Pause

The rhythm of our breath has three parts: the exhalation, the inhalation, and the pauses in between. A healthy, relaxed breath has a slight pause at the end of the exhalation where the breath seems to dissolve and disappear into silence. There is also a slight pause at the "top" of the inhalation, when the breath seems to be suspended within. In times of stress, we can lose the pauses in our breath—and also quite literally lose the "pauses" in our lives!

But allowing for pauses does not mean mechanically extending them. They happen as a natural result of learning to relax into the breath. And while some traditional yogic breathing techniques include retention of the breath, we do not encourage these for children.

Natural Breath Inquiry for Teens and Adults—An Exercise Encompassing All Five Healthy Breathing Principles

Sit in a chair or lie on your back with your knees bent and feet on floor. Rest one hand on your low belly and the other on your upper chest. Close your eyes. Breathe. Then consider:

- Where do you feel your breath? Is it in your upper or lower torso?

- Where does your breath originate?

- Can you hear your breath?

- Without changing your breath, notice what it feels like. Is it smooth or rough? Jerky or rhythmic? Slow or fast?

- Are your inhalations and exhalations the same length?

- Now begin to pay attention to your exhalation. Notice how your body naturally feels heavier when you exhale.

- Relax your muscles and let your awareness travel down the length of an exhalation. Do this several times and enjoy the sensation of breath effortlessly leaving the body. As you relax more, notice how your exhalations naturally lengthen.

- Notice the slight pause at the end of the breath before the new one comes in. Relax and enjoy the pause without changing it. Then notice how the next new breath rises naturally and wavelike from the belly.

- Afterward, notice that the natural diaphragmatic (belly) breath emerges after relaxing and that there is a balance of conscious control and letting go. This relaxed attentiveness is perfect for learning, sports, playing music—all of life's activities!

Yoga Calm Breath Techniques for Children

The Natural Breath Inquiry (above) requires a high level of cognitive development and concentration skills and would be appropriate for most teens and adults. For younger students and lower levels of cognitive development, a different approach is required.

Yoga Calm techniques for leading yogic breathing exercises with K-8 students are adapted for children's developmental level, as they have shorter attention spans and more difficulty grasping some subtle concepts. For them, a more "physical" or tangible breathing exercise is needed, helping them to see and synchronize their breath with movement.

Synchronized breathing in a group exercise is also useful, as we are affected by each other's breathing patterns. By learning to breathe together in a relaxed manner, we develop a sense of community and safety. Conversely, it is hard to relax and concentrate when we are around stressful breathing patterns. As you learn, practice, and model healthy breathing, your classes will be calmer and more productive, with corresponding benefits to everyone's health and well-being.

Yoga Calm uses five activities to bring awareness and control to breathing and develop healthy breathing habits:

1. Belly Breathing (p. 63), done in seated, standing, prone, and supine positions, helps children develop efficient and relaxed diaphragmatic breathing.

2. Volcano Breath (p. 97) establishes the pause at the top of the inhalation and helps slow exhalation. Employing an aspirant, breathy sound—like a volcano erupting—provides even more awareness of the breath and aids in slowing it down.

3. Pinwheel Breath (p. 81) aids in breath efficiency and further teaches how to slow the exhalation by using a pursed-lip technique.

4. Synchronizing the breath with movement in pose flows, Arm Swings (p. 60), and other physical activities prevents breath holding, encourages more natural movement, and provides opportunities to practice staying relaxed while being challenged.

5. Finally, Back Breathing (p. 61) in either a seated position or the Child pose (p. 70) aids in relaxation and develops trust.

You will find complete descriptions of all of these activities in the following chapter.

Yoga Calm Tools
Yoga-Based Activities | 5

In general, children today are much less active than kids of even a generation ago. It seems that not a week goes by without at least one news story calling our attention to the problems—such as obesity—that result from inactivity and emphasizing the need for kids to get moving. And yet, paradoxically, there are also reports of hyperactive children—of children who just can't seem to sit still. What's needed for both of these extremes is meaningful movement—physical activity that's combined with processes that fully engage the mind and emotions. This integrative approach is at the heart of all Yoga Calm activities and can be seen through its goals:

1. Develop safe, accessible, and enjoyable lifelong physical fitness habits for students and teachers of all ages and abilities.

2. Reduce stress and develop physical fitness, strength, flexibility, and balance, as well as self-awareness, self-regulation, concentration, and social and emotional skills.

3. Support learning preparedness with activities that create an optimum level of arousal for learning.

4. Support emotional and cognitive skill development through greater organization of the sensory system.

5. Develop the Yoga Calm wellness principles of Stillness, Listening, Grounding, Strength, and Community.

6. Support academic learning by providing opportunities to integrate Yoga Calm activities with other educational curricula and lesson plans.

The long-term benefits of a wellness practice like yoga are built upon the development of safe, healthy habits. Thus, we are particularly grateful to the Iyengar yoga tradition, and especially our teacher Julie Gudmestad for their emphasis on safety and alignment. Their guidance has helped us develop practices that have supported our own health and, through our own teachings, the health of thousands of students. Based on this foundation and on our experience in teaching children's yoga, we have created the following alignment and safety guidelines for teaching Yoga Calm activities.

Integrative Alignment: General Principles

In teaching yoga to children, we have found three general alignment principles to be most useful: Breathe, Activate, and Expand.

Breathe

In every yoga pose, breathe in a full and relaxed manner—just as in the Belly Breathing activity discussed in the previous chapter. If the breath is held, shallow, erratic, or strained, the pose is either misaligned or too advanced for the student, or the student is making too much effort. But by observing changes in the breath, we can develop awareness of when we are under stress. Being able to breathe easily, and through the nose, counterbalances the beginner's tendency to strain. It also provides more oxygen to working muscles and calms the nervous system.

You can experience the synergistic relationship between breath and alignment by coming to a sitting position with your head and shoulders slumped forward. Breathe shallowly at first. How does this feel? What does this posture communicate? Then breathe more fully. Do you notice how these fuller inhalations tend to raise your head and shoulders? It's as if your breath is telling you to sit more upright! Now, gradually lift your head and take your shoulders back with each full inhalation until your head is upright and your shoulders are back and over the hips. How does this feel?

While the air we breathe in extends only to the boundaries of the rib cage, the energy, action, and molecules of the breath naturally radiate throughout the body. Poor alignment can interfere with the breath, and shallow and constrained breathing does not support good posture—a vicious cycle. Conversely, aligning the body properly facilitates breathing, and helps us "remember" good alignment. Thus, proper breathing encourages your fullest form, and aligning your body properly encourages your deepest breath.

Activate

You activate your body by firming the muscles in toward their bones and drawing the limbs toward the centerline of your body. The centerline is the body's anatomical middle. It corresponds to the spine and an imaginary line that extends out the top of the head and tip of the tailbone, and our bodies constantly orient to it. This is most evident when we're standing, as we align our body's centerline (spine) to the line of gravity.

This integrative action of drawing to the centerline helps our balance, stabilizes the joints, and protects the muscles, tendons, and ligaments. It also provides physical self-awareness and a sense of security. One of the reasons Mountain (p. 79) is one of the first poses taught in classical yoga is that it develops this midline awareness and our ability to "hug into" our center. Other good poses and activities for teaching the Activation principle include Activate/Relax Walk (p. 58), Tree (p. 91), and Star with hugging-in action (p. 88).

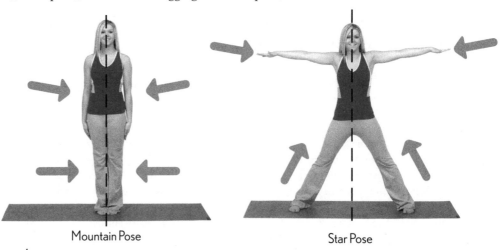

Mountain Pose   Star Pose

Expand

To expand out from the center of the body, press all points of the body—arms, legs, top of the head, chest, tailbone, and so on—away from the centerline. Such movement aligns, lengthens, and decompresses the joints and musculoskeletal system. It engages the intrinsic postural muscles that align and lengthen the spine. It helps with balance and stability, and provides another way to reference the body's center. It simultaneously provides physical self-awareness and a proud, expansive sense of self.

Perhaps the single best illustration of the Expansion principle comes from Leonardo da Vinci's classic Ventruvian Man, which shows both the action and the sense of holism that results from an enlarged sense of self. Good activities to teach this principle to your students include Star (p. 88), Upward Mountain (p. 96), Warrior I (p. 98), and Warrior II (p. 99).

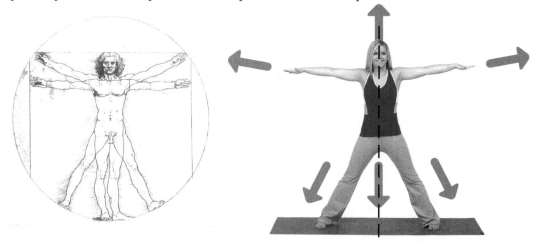

Star Pose

Integrating the Principles

Activating and Expanding at the same time has complementary effects on physical and emotional levels. It keeps your students from becoming too rigid or overextended—and it provides an emotional experience of safety combined with an expansive sense of self.

A useful metaphor for describing these complementary forces is the sun. Its incredibly strong gravitational pull keeps Earth and the other planets from flying out of orbit. At the same time, it supports a nuclear reaction that sends energy in all directions for billions of miles.

All three alignment principles can be effectively represented by breathing fully in and out along with the expanding and contracting actions of a Hoberman Sphere. You experience the pulling to the middle, the expansion outward, and deep, relaxed breathing.

Refining Alignment: Anatomical Landmarks

In addition to teaching the three alignment principles above, how do you recognize and encourage good alignment in yoga poses? The following are a few key anatomical landmarks and how to teach their alignment actions. Knowledge of these landmarks and their actions, illustrated with the photographs of specific poses in the following section, will further enable you to safely guide students into the poses.

Hands

Spread the fingers and press out through the fingertips and four corners of the hand. Have each child use a finger to trace a square around his or her own hand, outlining the edges of the palm. When in poses like Downward Dog (p. 74) and Plank (p. 82), in which the hands hold one's weight, keep the weight off the wrists by pressing down through the fingertips and the palm knuckles (where the fingers and palm meet).

Downward Dog

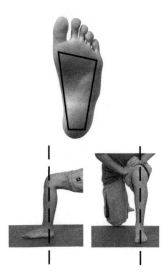

Feet

Spread the toes and press out evenly through the four corners of each foot. Have each child use a finger to trace a rectangle around his or her foot, outlining the edges and corners of the sole. This awareness of the feet can be further developed through use of the analogy of a chair with its four stable legs in the Roots activity (p. 85). It can also be taught through any of the standing poses.

Knees

In standing poses such as Side Angle (p. 87) and Warrior I (p. 98), in which the knee is bent toward a right angle, bring the knee out until it is positioned right over the top of the ankle and not tipping to either side. This prevents a shearing force on the knee joint.

Sitting Bones

When sitting, press down through the sitting bones to lengthen the spine. In all poses, taking the sitting bones slightly back will seat the thigh bone more deeply into the hip socket and help maintain a healthy inward curve in the low back.

Top of Head and Tailbone

At opposite ends of the spine are the head and tailbone. The basic alignment action of these two landmarks is to press them away from each other. The lengthening of the tailbone is initiated with a gentle forward-scooping action.

Abdomen

Engage the lower abdominal muscles without making them hard. This action works in conjunction with the lengthening of the tailbone and helps initiate the stabilizing action of the core abdominal and pelvic muscles.

Chest

Lift the upper chest. This action promotes a lengthening of the spine and healthy shoulder alignment.

Shoulders

Move the top of the arm bones (where they meet the shoulders) toward the back of the body. Draw the shoulder blades onto the back and into the back of the heart, supporting the lift of the chest.

Please refer to the bibliography for additional sources on proper yoga alignment.

Warrior I

Use Language to Align from the Inside Out

Alignment will be easier and more desirable for students when you use simple, evocative, descriptive language that conveys an attitude of alignment (e.g., "Stand tall and proud.") or a quality of being (e.g., "Imagine you are a king or queen with a crown on your head."). For example, note the difference in saying "Press your feet down and lift your arms up" versus saying "Root your feet into the earth and touch the sky!" Here are some more examples of language that evokes a positive attitude and proper alignment:

- Activate like a superhero.
- Extend laser beams from your fingertips.
- Think of someone you are strong for.
- Lift your head like you are wearing antlers.

An even more powerful kind of instruction is to link an alignment principle with both a physical landmark and an image or quality of being. This helps integrate the physical action of a pose with a corresponding emotional and cognitive experience. For example, saying "Press out through the top of your head like you are wearing a crown" combines the alignment principle of Expansion, the top-of-head physical landmark, and the cognitive image and emotional quality of sovereignty.

Teaching in this way can be very creative and fun. Imagine a comprehensive lesson that includes a theme like the king or queen archetype, poses and language that convey those qualities, and a related story, writing, or art project. This integrative approach to teaching is more efficient, accomplishes many goals, and is ultimately more meaningful and effective than standard methods. And when yoga is taught this way, it becomes more than just a purely physical pursuit. It becomes a tool for a lifetime of self-discovery and development.

The activity pages that follow illustrate the alignment principles described above and provide recommended methods for teaching Yoga Calm's physical poses and activities. We also give variations on the activities and ideas for integrating them with classroom lesson plans.

To find activities quickly and develop class plans to meet your specific needs, look to the icons in the upper outer corner of each page. The first icon designates the primary Yoga Calm principle embodied in that activity, while the others indicate additional principles expressed through it.

| Stillness | Listening | Grounding | Strength | Community |

ACTIVATE/ RELAX WALK

BENEFITS

Develops self-regulation, focus, and ability to follow directions, make transitions, and shift attention. A good warm-up activity accessible to a wide range of students. Teaches relaxed concentration necessary for testing.

TIME

2 to 5 minutes

ACTIVITY

- Have student demonstrate Mountain and how to Activate (firm muscles and focus attention).

- Students walk around the room in a relaxed manner. Upon Activate command, students freeze, firm, and focus; upon Relax command, they continue walking.

- Alternate commands back and forth—Activate, Relax, Activate, Relax— giving a few seconds for each.

- After several cycles, ask students to walk in a way that is *both* Activated and Relaxed.

VARIATIONS & INTEGRATION

- Add various poses to the Activate command—for example, going from Relaxed walk to Warrior II (p. 99) or Tree (p. 91).

- For better classroom management and with physically challenged students, start activity from a chair, alternately contracting and relaxing muscles.

- Use with health lesson about body posture (see Mountain, p. 79).

- Discuss situations in which students need to be Relaxed (e.g., resting), Activated (e.g., near an angry dog), and both Relaxed and Activated together (e.g., athletics, performing arts, sitting in class, testing).

NOTES

See also Mat Tag (p. 78).

ALTERNATE ARM/LEG KICKS

BENEFITS

Energizes and warms body. Develops core strength, postural muscles, and balance. Activates and integrates both hemispheres of the brain. Develops cross-lateral coordination and outer hip stability necessary for walking. Accessible to a wide range of students.

TIME

10 to 20 seconds each side

ACTIVITY

- Come to all fours with hands under shoulders and knees under hips.
- Stretch right leg straight back and point toes down. Hips and leg are level with floor.
- Now, lift and lengthen left arm, with thumb pointing up.
- Look slightly down, lift belly, and lengthen from top of head to tail.
- Keep hips and body still for 5 to 10 seconds. Extended leg and arm stay horizontal and parallel to floor.
- Switch sides, lifting left leg and right arm.

VARIATIONS & INTEGRATION

- Lift opposite arm and leg in unison for greater integration of brain hemispheres.
- While in pose, take raised arm and leg out to the side and then back, squeezing into the midline.
- For those who have trouble kneeling, substitute Superman (see p. 89).

NOTES

Because most mental processes involve both sides of the brain, integration problems between the two hemispheres can result in inefficiencies in brain processes. Thus, some children with reading difficulties, central auditory processing disorders, language delay, and other learning problems may be suffering from a lack of hemispheric integration. This activity activates and integrates both hemispheres of the brain. Research indicates that this integration is related to ease of learning to read for school-age children.

This activity also can help with underdeveloped postural (extensor) muscles that can result from the amount of time children and babies spend sitting and on their backs.

ARM SWINGS

BENEFITS

Quick, simple, and effective group activity that energizes, oxygenates, and stimulates. Helpful before a test or when students are sluggish or have been sitting too long. Good integration of breath, movement, and positive self-talk. Develops group awareness and sensitivity.

TIME

1 to 2 minutes

ACTIVITY

- From standing, inhale and turn palms outward and raise your arms out to the side and then overhead.
- Exhale and lower your arms back to your sides.
- Let the movement of your arms follow your breath.
- See how slowly and smoothly you can move, like a bird flying in slow motion.

VARIATIONS & INTEGRATION

- Add positive self-talk phrases to the up-and-down movements of the arms such as "I am strong. I am in control. I can do it. I can be responsible."
- For a quick, relaxing, yet energizing group activity before a test, combine Belly Breathing (p. 63) with the Hoberman Sphere, Arm Swings, and Shoulder Clock (p. 86).

NOTES

Long periods of sitting hunched over negatively affect posture, breathing, quality of attention, and health of the shoulders and upper back. OSHA standards now recommend at least 10 minutes of movement per hour of sitting.

See also Volcano Breath (p. 97) and Chair (p. 69).

BACK BREATHING

BENEFITS

Calms and relaxes. Develops trust and ability to give and receive. Develops sensitivity and compassion for others. A good activity when students are afraid or need emotional support.

TIME

2 to 5 minutes

ACTIVITY

- One student takes Child pose (p. 70) while another kneels alongside and places their hands on the first student's low back.
- The student in the Child pose breathes slowly into the low back and into the partner's hands, feeling the hands rise and fall like waves in an ocean, or like a parachute or sail filling with air.
- Continue for several breaths. Move hands up to midback and repeat.
- Continue for several breaths; then move hands to upper back (shoulder blade area) and repeat.
- Switch roles.

VARIATIONS & INTEGRATION

- To develop trust and prepare for this activity, use Back Drawing (p. 62) first.
- Combine with lesson on appropriate touch.
- Combine with health lesson about the spine's role in supporting the body or about what it means to feel supported in life.
- Use to teach anatomy of the back body by working in pairs to palpate the shoulder blades, spine, rib cage, kidney area, and so on.

NOTES

People unconsciously synchronize with each other from many sources including nonverbal cues, emotional energy, and breathing. Watching and feeling another person breathe slowly and deeply helps students to calm, slow their breath, and develop sensitivity and compassion.

If students do not want to be touched, allow them to watch and synchronize with another's breathing as if watching Hoberman Sphere activity (see Belly Breathing, p. 63).

BACK DRAWING

BENEFITS

Calms and relaxes. Develops trust and ability to give and take. A great group exercise and a good reward.

TIME

10 to 15 minutes

ACTIVITY

- Stand in a close circle, turn to the right, and sit in a cross-legged position. (This can also be done in chairs.)
- Place hands on the back of the person in front of you.
- Begin by making rain on the person's back—gently tapping the back.
- Now, make it rain all the way down the back—fingers sliding gently down the back.
- Then, make very light thunder—gently tapping the back.
- Then, lightning—draw lightning strikes.
- Now, draw big, puffy rain clouds.
- Brush those clouds away—gently sweeping hands across the back.
- Now the sun comes out—draw a big sun with a happy face and sunglasses!
- Place palms on the back in front of you. Close eyes and feel the warm hands of the person behind you. Imagine yourself in a beautiful or favorite place with the sun warming your back.
- When the sun comes out, the flowers begin to grow—draw a beautiful flower for your friend.
- Now draw either a gift or a secret message on the other person's back. Whisper into the person's ear what the gift or secret message is.

VARIATIONS & INTEGRATION

- Create imagery on the back that relates to a specific time of year, current event, or academic theme such as holidays, snow, a parade, or a nature scene.
- Have students share what gifts they gave and received, or the messages they sent to one another.
- After drawing the gift or message on the back, have each student draw the image on paper or write down the message so they can remember it.
- For students who are sensitive to touch, try "short-stroking," an occupational therapy technique that uses alternating palm pressure down the spine with one hand starting before the first stops.
- Other options for students sensitive to touch are to use firmer pressure or let them sit and watch the group.

NOTES

This activity works well for virtually all students and is a great family activity. Children request this activity all the time!

For older students, a group shoulder massage in a circle is a special treat before or after a test—or for a relaxation break. With teenage students, it works best if boys and girls form their own circles. Also, you can use more sophisticated imagery.

BELLY BREATHING: SEATED, STANDING, OR PRONE

BENEFITS

Calms, focuses, and helps to self-regulate. Oxygenates the body. Teaches healthy, diaphragmatic breathing and draws awareness inward.

TIME

1 to 2 minutes

ACTIVITY

- Students lie on their backs, stand, or sit in a chair with feet on the ground, hip-width apart. Hands are placed on the belly.
- Breathe into your belly so that hands go up and down with the breath like waves in the ocean.
- Relax all muscles to slow the breath even further.

VARIATIONS & INTEGRATION

- Have a student demonstrate deep breathing while expanding and contracting the Hoberman Sphere as the class follows. This also develops group awareness and students' sensitivity to each other.
- Keeping one hand on the belly, bring the other hand up to the chest. Breathe from belly hand to heart hand.
- From seated position, place both palms on low back above hips. Breathe into the low back and hands (similar to Back Breathing, p. 61).
- From supine position, place a small flat stone or object on the belly. Move the object up and down with the breath.
- Take Pulse Count (p. 83) before and after Belly Breathing, and then do both at the same time to notice the relationship between breath and pulse.
- Use in health lessons on stress. Have students notice what happens to their breath during daily activities and when they are under stress.
- Use the imagery or sounds of slow-moving waves or wind to help slow the mind and breathing.
- Use slow, relaxing music (50 to 60 beats per minute).
- Teach a lesson or read a story about oxygen and why it is so important to the body.
- Anatomy inquiry: "Do you know what your lungs look like? Do you know where they are? What bones protect the lungs? What is your diaphragm?" Expand inquiry into the importance of clean air and protecting the environment.

NOTES

Even though the lungs physically extend only from under the collarbones to the lowest ribs, the abdominal organs move down and out with the diaphragm's action to help draw air into the body, giving the appearance and the sense that we are breathing into the belly.

Relaxed, diaphragmatic breathing has a positive effect on the cardiovascular, neurological, gastrointestinal, and muscular systems, and has a general effect on sleep, memory, energy levels, and concentration. For more information, see chapter 4.

BLOCK CREEK

BENEFITS

Develops focus and balance. Helps students develop ability to stay focused when others are challenging or distracting them.

TIME

20 minutes

ACTIVITY

- Line up two yoga mats end to end, making one long mat approximately 12 feet long.
- Stagger yoga blocks down the length of the mats, approximately one foot apart.
- Imagine the blocks are rocks across a creek, with the mat being the water.
- Walk slowly down the blocks from one end to the other without falling.
- Go slowly, look, and step carefully on each "rock."
- Bend your knees and imagine that your weight drops into your feet.
- Try it again, this time looking straight ahead, not looking at the rocks. Another student can stand at the end of the mat to help you focus.

VARIATIONS & INTEGRATION

- Use positive self-talk such as "I am strong" or "I can do it."
- After students have mastered the first task, have them walk Block Creek with their eyes closed, with the help of a partner guide on each side.
- Have them balance an object or a basket on their head as they cross the creek.
- Have "trolls" in the water that growl at them and try to throw them off (no touching) as they cross the creek.
- Have students pretend they are crossing a swift river. When a student steps off the block, they are out of the game. This will slow down students who go across too quickly.
- Invite students to share strategies they used to get across the creek.
- Integrate with a lesson plan on harassment.
- At the end of the session, lead a Guided Relaxation (chapter 7) that includes a river or crossing a creek.

NOTES

To prepare for Block Creek, use Dancer (p. 72), Roots (p. 85), Tree (p. 91), and other balance poses.

Have students move slowly, safely, and under control. Use partners to help support students with balance issues or if you are in doubt of a student's ability.

This activity develops focus and peripheral vision to help children be less triggered by peripheral distractions.

Occupational therapists can substitute the round, squishy half-hemispheres they use instead of yoga blocks.

BOAT

BENEFITS

Energizes. Quickly warms the body. Develops balance and strength in abdominal muscles, legs, and back.

TIME

A few seconds to 1 minute

ACTIVITY

- Sit on the floor. Bend knees toward chest. Grab backs of thighs and balance on sitting bones.
- Lift low back, heart, and head.
- Pull shoulders back.
- While holding backs of legs, alternately stretch one leg straight, then the other, then both.
- Very challenging: keep legs straight, stretch arms out straight and parallel to floor, or even overhead.
- In all variations, keep breathing and lifting up the low back.
- Full pose will look like the front view of a boat, with the legs and upper body the same distance from floor (not listing to one side or the other).

VARIATIONS & INTEGRATION

- Practice with knees bent and hands holding backs of legs first, especially if hamstrings are tight and/or low back rounds toward floor.

NOTES

Tight hamstring muscles can limit the ability to do this pose. Therefore, use this pose after children are warmed up, with knees bent if necessary, and preferably after some preliminary hamstring stretches like Leg Extensions (p. 77) or Forward Bend (p. 76).

BOW

BENEFITS

Stretches the entire front of the body. Strengthens the back muscles. Improves posture. Massages the abdominal organs.

TIME

20 to 30 seconds

ACTIVITY

- Lie on your belly.
- Bend knees, reach back and grab ankles.
- Pull knees toward each other so they are hip-width apart.
- Inhale, press feet back, lift chest and head up off the floor.
- Look forward and lengthen from top of head to tail.
- Keep breathing! Imagine your breath filling your back.

VARIATIONS & INTEGRATION

- Keep holding your ankles as you roll all the way over onto one side and then the other.
- Rock forward and back like a cradle.

NOTES

Like Cobra (p. 71) and Superman (p. 89), Bow strengthens the diaphragm/respiratory muscles and is a great antidote to the stress of sitting for long periods of time.

BRIDGE

BENEFITS

Energizes. Strengthens the back body (hamstrings, gluteals, shoulder blade muscles) and stretches the front body. Good for posture and grounding.

TIME

20 seconds to 1 minute

ACTIVITY

- Lie on back with feet flat on floor, close to hips, hip-width apart, toes pointing straight ahead.
- Pull elbows in close to ribs and point fingers toward sky ("robot arms").
- Breathe in, activate arms ("robot arms"), and lift heart by pressing shoulders and elbows toward floor.
- Breathe out, lift tailbone, and press down through the feet and shoulders to lift hips and heart up to the sky.
- Keep thighs parallel and press down the four corners of each foot.
- Tip head slightly back to open the throat and breathe more fully.
- Hold pose for two to three breaths.
- To come out, keep tailbone lifted and roll the spine down to the floor from upper back to hips.
- Do pose three times in a row.

VARIATIONS & INTEGRATION

- Drawbridge imagery: Exhale as you lift the bridge up. As you hold the pose and continue to breathe, let imaginary boats go under the bridge. Exhale as you lower the bridge.
- Hold a yoga block between the knees to develop more core strength and to keep knees from splaying out to the sides.
- Keep thighs parallel and one foot flat on floor while stretching the other leg out straight and parallel to floor. Repeat with the other leg.

NOTES

Keep all four corners of the foot on the ground (particularly the inner foot). Practice drawing the four corners of the foot before doing pose. (See Alignment, p. 56.)

This activity strengthens and warms up hamstring muscles, preparing them for stretching, and is good preparation for Bow (p. 66) and Table (p. 90). It can help also with underdeveloped postural (extensor) muscles that can result from the amount of time children and babies spend sitting and on their backs.

CAT/COW

BENEFITS

Gently warms the body while stretching the spine and rib cage. Assists with complete inhalation and exhalation, slows breathing, integrates breath and movement by synchronizing the spine's natural articulation with the breath. Also takes the spine through the complete range of flexion and extension.

TIME

30 seconds to 1 minute

ACTIVITY

- Come to all fours with hands under shoulders and knees under hips.
- Breathe out, lower head, and tuck tail. Your back will round up like a cat's.
- Breathe in, look up, and lift head and collarbones. Your belly will drop like a cow's.
- Breathe smoothly and slowly, moving from Cat to Cow and matching the motion with the breath.
- Make Cat and Cow motions of equal duration, inhaling and exhaling the same length of time.

VARIATIONS & INTEGRATION

- Dog Chasing Its Tail: Make a big side bend by looking over shoulder toward one hip and then the other. Inhale bending to one side, exhale back to center, inhale to other side, exhale back to center. Try to keep the hips centered over the knees to encourage more side body length.
- Preface Cat/Cow with a Hoberman Sphere breathing exercise (see Belly Breathing, p. 63) to help students with synchronizing breath and movement.

CHAIR

BENEFITS

Quickly warms and energizes the body. Strengthens the ankles, thighs, calves, spine, and shoulders. Accessible to a wide range of abilities.

TIME

30 seconds to 1 minute

ACTIVITY

- Stand with legs hip-width apart, as in Mountain (p. 79).
- Inhale and raise and straighten arms overhead, keeping arms parallel with palms facing each other, as in Upward Mountain (p. 96).
- Exhale, bend knees, and take thighs back as if sitting in an imaginary chair.
- Keep knees in alignment with feet (not knock-kneed or bowlegged).
- Point feet straight ahead (no duck or pigeon feet!) and press down the four corners of each foot.
- Lift the belly, head, and heart.
- Feel your strength!
- To come out of pose, breathe in, press down through the feet, and reach up to the sky while gradually lengthening and straightening your legs.
- Finish in Mountain pose.

VARIATIONS & INTEGRATION

- Use Arm Swings (p. 60) as a warm-up activity.
- Add positive self-talk—"I am strong. I can do it."—with movements.
- Combine with Strong Voice activity (p. 122).

NOTES

One of the quickest and safest ways to warm the body.

CHILD

BENEFITS

Calms the nervous system and helps relieve stress and fatigue. Good resting pose between more challenging poses. Inward turning action invites introspection and rest.

TIME

30 seconds to a few minutes

ACTIVITY

- Kneel on the floor. With the tops of the feet on the floor, touch the big toes together and sit back on the heels.
- Stack hands on the floor to make a pillow, or pull arms alongside body.
- Relax your neck, hips, and back. Let your head be heavy.
- Breathe into your back and let it puff up like a parachute.

VARIATIONS & INTEGRATION

- If you have difficulty sitting on your heels in this pose, place a blanket between your thighs and calves, or sit back on a yoga block.
- Seated version: Sitting in a chair, lean forward and hang head and arms down toward the floor. You can also make a pillow with forearms on a desk or the back of a chair, to rest the head.
- Add One-Minute Exploration (p. 134).
- Child pose is good preparation for Back Breathing (p. 61).

NOTES

Child pose is similar to the fetal position, an instinctual posture to protect the brain and vital organs.

COBRA

BENEFITS

Energizes. Stretches front body while strengthening core and postural muscles. Develops focus. Good integration of breath, movement, and group awareness.

TIME

10 to 20 seconds

ACTIVITY

- Lie on belly with tops of feet on floor and legs close together.
- Place palms flat on floor and under shoulders. Fingers point straight ahead. Press four corners of hands (p. 55) down.
- Make a slow hissing sound and lift head, heart, and belly.
- Keep shoulders back and down, elbows close to body, tops of feet on floor.
- Lower and repeat two more times.

VARIATIONS & INTEGRATION

- Make the hissing sound a whisper.
- Try the pose with hands off the floor, along the sides, or clasped behind the back so students use their core muscles and their breath more to support lift.
- Instead of pushing their way up into the pose, have students pull their heart forward and up while keeping the shoulders back and down and elbows slightly bent and close to ribs.

NOTES

Children need good "tummy time" to develop the back body's extensor muscles—key muscles for postural support. Like the action of Alternate Arm/ Leg Kicks (p. 59) and Superman (p. 89), Cobra supports the development of these key muscles and movements.

DANCER
MODIFIED

BENEFITS

Calms, clears, and focuses the mind. Develops concentration, stability, strength, and grounding. Good after sitting for long periods and in preparation for tests. A balance pose that can be done by almost everyone.

TIME

10 seconds to 1 minute

ACTIVITY

- Stand with feet hip-width apart.
- Shift weight to the right foot. Lift the left foot behind and hold it with left hand.
- When in balance, raise the right arm.
- Look straight ahead. Focus on a spot on the wall to help with balance.
- Repeat on other side.

VARIATIONS & INTEGRATION

- To prepare for Dancer, balance on one foot at a time with eyes open and with eyes closed.
- Time students. Lengthen holding time as they grow stronger.
- Imagine a loved one holding your standing foot to the ground.
- Use positive self-talk: "I am strong. I am in control. I can do it."
- Have students visualize themselves as superheroes as they balance.
- Have students close their eyes in the pose.
- Good pose to practice before more challenging balance activities like Block Creek (p. 64) or Tree Challenge (p. 92).
- Ask students to "Activate" and "Relax" (see p. 58) while they're in the pose, then share their experiences.
- Have students practice changing images in their minds—visualizing a tall tree, a rock, and so on—and notice whether it has an effect on their balance.

NOTES

Prolonged sitting can tighten the thigh and hip flexor muscles. This pose counteracts that, while also providing quiet and deep proprioceptive stimulation.

By age 5, most children should be able to balance on one foot for 10 seconds.

DOLPHIN

BENEFITS

Builds whole-body strength, especially abdominal muscles, arms, and shoulders.

TIME

10 seconds to 1 minute

ACTIVITY

- Place elbows shoulder-width apart on the floor. Interlace hands tightly and press them down.
- Look up slightly and lift chest up and away from the floor.
- Turn toes under, lift hips, and straighten legs as in Downward Dog (p. 74).
- Keep the head and heart lifting while moving forward to a planklike position, then back to a hips-lifted position.
- Keep breaths slow and relaxed.
- Repeat three or four times.

VARIATIONS & INTEGRATION

- For an easier pose, keep knees on the floor but make the same action, forward and back, heart and head lifting.
- Use positive self-talk: "I am strong. I am in control. I can do it."

NOTES

Strong core muscles (abdominals and in the hips and low back) help with posture, prevent injuries, and contribute to a sense of competency in the world.

To prepare for Dolphin, use Downward Dog (p. 74) or Plank (p. 82) and its variations.

DOWNWARD DOG

BENEFITS

Energizes, calms, and strengthens. Increases flexibility in shoulders, hips, and backs of legs. Deeply seats the leg and arm bones into their sockets, providing a sense of integration. Weight-bearing through arms and upper body stimulates development of strong, healthy bones.

TIME

5 seconds to 2 minutes

ACTIVITY

- Come to all fours with hands under shoulders and knees under and slightly behind hips.
- Point fingers straight ahead and spread them like rays of the sun.
- Press down through the four corners of the hands and feet.
- Activate and straighten arms.
- Turn toes under and press thighs and hips toward wall behind you, creating an "A" shape.
- Keep arms straight with head and chest slightly lifting up to create a flat back from head to hips.
- Knees can be slightly bent to keep back from rounding up.

VARIATIONS & INTEGRATION

- Time the pose, and as students get stronger, lengthen the time they hold.
- Chair Dog: Use the back or seat of a chair or a table to adapt pose or for classroom use.
- Heel Pumps: Inhale and lift heels up; exhale and lower heels.
- Alternate going from Downward Dog to Plank (p. 82) and back. Keep belly, head, and heart lifting up.
- Leg Lifts: Inhale and lift one leg up, away from the floor and in a line with arms and upper body. Keep arms straight, lift belly, and press out strongly through the four corners of the raised foot. Hold for 5 to 10 seconds; exhale the foot back to the floor. Repeat with the other leg.
- Walk hands back to feet to come into Forward Bend (p. 76).

NOTES

Children can have tight hamstrings, resulting in upwardly rounded backs in this pose. To take the strain off the lower back, have them look up, bend their knees slightly, and press their thighs back.

The inverted nature of this pose facilitates a complete exhalation, activates the vestibular system, and helps to calm the nervous system.

Stretching the calf muscles helps prevent common sports injuries.

EAGLE

BENEFITS

Grounds, calms, and activates the brain. Develops bilateral skills and balance. Strengthens legs and hips. Increases flexibility in ankles, hips, and shoulders. Good for students with attention difficulties.

TIME

15 to 30 seconds

ACTIVITY

- From standing, bend knees slightly, as in Chair (p. 69).
- Lift your left leg off the floor and cross your left knee tightly over right knee.
- Hug your foot into your shin or hook the toes of your left foot behind your right calf.
- Spread your arms like wings and take them overhead.
- Bend your elbows and hook your left elbow under your right elbow in front of your heart.
- Point your thumbs toward your nose and grab your right palm with your left hand, or place backs of hands together.
- Lift elbows up and stretch your fingers toward the sky.
- Repeat on other side.

VARIATIONS & INTEGRATION

- Eagle on a Cliff: While in the pose, imagine you are an eagle perched on a cliff. While still balancing on one foot, unhook your arms, "open your wings," unwind your top leg and stretch it back. Imagine yourself flying. And then come back to your perch (Eagle pose) again without touching your foot down.

NOTES

Cross-motor activities have been used to activate the brain since our understanding of laterality began more than a century ago. Noted authorities such as Orton, Doman, Delacato, Kephart, Barsch, and Dennison (Brain Gym) have successfully used similar movements in their learning programs.

To prepare for Eagle on a Cliff, use Brain Gym Hook-Ups and cross crawl activities like Alternate Arm/Leg Kicks (p. 59).

FORWARD BEND

BENEFITS

Calms and releases tension. Stretches hamstrings, calves, and hips. Invites introspection and rest.

TIME

A few seconds to a few minutes

ACTIVITY

- Place feet hip-width apart and point them straight ahead (no duck or pigeon feet).
- Bend at the hips and hang arms, head, and spine toward the floor (like a rag doll).
- Touch the floor with your fingers. If your fingers don't reach, bend your knees. Imagine your back, head, and arms flowing down like a waterfall.
- Breathe into your back.
- To come out of the pose, bend knees, place hands on hips, look up, and stand as in Chair (p. 69).

VARIATIONS & INTEGRATION

- Keeping fingers on floor, inhale, lift head and heart, then exhale and lower back down.
- To deepen pose, press feet down and lengthen legs.
- With support: lean forward and place forearms and head on your desk or the chair in front of you.
- While students are in Forward Bend, talk to them about the importance of turning their awareness inward.

NOTES

This pose and Leg Extensions (p. 77) help to prevent hamstring strains, a common injury with athletes.

Avoid this pose if low back or knee pain results.

LEG EXTENSIONS/ FOOT CIRCLES

BENEFITS

Stretches hips, hamstrings, and calves. Promotes ankle strength and range of motion. Helps with posture and health of low back.

TIME

10 to 30 seconds each leg

ACTIVITY

- Lie on back and stretch right leg up into the air.
- Interlace hands behind your right thigh.
- Straighten both legs as much as possible, right leg into air and left leg flat on the floor.
- Draw circles with your right foot in one direction and then the other. Keep the rest of the leg still.
- Switch legs and repeat.

VARIATIONS & INTEGRATION

- Expand on foot circles (and time in pose) by writing or spelling your name or even the whole alphabet with your big toe.
- Use a strap over the sole of the raised foot to hold the leg up and stretch the calf muscles.
- Balance a block on your foot. Press it up toward the ceiling and keep it level with the floor.

NOTES

Foot circles are good for ankle flexibility—important for balance and injury prevention—and prolong the time necessary for the hamstring muscles to stretch. Flexibility in ankles, calves, and hamstrings is important to prevent injury in sports activities.

MAT TAG

BENEFITS

Develops focus and ability to follow directions, make transitions, and shift attention. Teaches turn-taking and ability to lead and follow. A good warm-up activity accessible to a wide range of students.

TIME

2 to 5 minutes

ACTIVITY

- In an open room, place several yoga mats 2 feet apart from each other.
- Play like traditional tag, but with students having to stay on the mats. Once tagged, the "It" student announces they are "It" by yelling *"Freeze."* Then they announce what speed the game is to be played at, *Slow, Medium* or *Fast.* If other students don't follow instructions (e.g., step off the mats or continue moving), they have to stand off the mats in Tree Pose for 5 seconds.

VARIATIONS & INTEGRATION

- As a discussion and turn-taking exercise, have students create their own commands and variations (*e.g., Backwards, Hopping, Sideways, Super Slow*).

NOTES

This can be a great activity before the beginning of a yoga class while waiting for all students to arrive or when students need to burn off some energy. It helps students to learn how to stop and calm themselves when excited. It also helps establish the yoga mat as a personal or protected space, as specified in the Yoga Calm Ground Rules (p. 42).

See also Activate/Relax Walk (p. 58).

MOUNTAIN

BENEFITS

Grounds, strengthens, and centers. Develops focus and postural awareness. Good beginning pose for new students.

TIME

1 to 2 minutes

ACTIVITY

- Stand with feet hip-width apart, pointing straight ahead, and press them down into the earth. Hands can be alongside the body, or palms together at heart.
- Lift belly, head, and heart. Shoulders are back and down.
- Look straight ahead.
- Body is Activated (firmed toward the centerline).

VARIATIONS & INTEGRATION

- Ask students to press their feet into the ground in order to lift the top of their head toward the sky: "Feel the strength and stability of the mountain inside."
- Have students stand with head and shoulders slumped versus standing in Mountain. Discuss how these different postures feel and what they communicate to others.
- Have students test the difference in stability between a feet-together stance versus hip-width Activated stance by gently pressing each other's shoulders from the side.
- Combine with Strong Voice activity (p. 122).
- Encourage students to close their eyes while performing the pose and think of someone they are strong for. Then invite students to share their thoughts.
- Provide photos of famous mountains to help students develop imagery and connect them to places in the world. Try being Mount Everest or Mount Fuji, then find those mountains on the map.
- Use the mountain theme through a sequence of standing poses. End with a Guided Relaxation (chapter 7) that includes visiting a mountaintop.

NOTES

Mountain is traditionally taught as one of the first yoga poses.

See Alignment (p. 54).

Over time, poor posture, with head and shoulders slumped forward, can result in neck, shoulder, and low back problems. Mountain supports good posture.

PARTNER PULL

BENEFITS

A fun partner activity that stretches the hips, low back, and shoulders. Opens side ribs for a fuller breath.

TIME

1 to 2 minutes

ACTIVITY

- Pair up and hold each other's right wrist with right hand.
- Step back about 1 to 2 feet, bend knees, and sit back until thighs are almost parallel to the floor and the back is flat.
- Gently pull the right hip back, stretching the right side body from shoulder to hip.
- Breathe in and fan the ribs out to the right in a side-bending action.
- Come up together.
- Repeat on the other side.

VARIATIONS & INTEGRATION

- Grab both hands and take both hips back.
- Teeter-totter: Grab both hands and come into a squatting position. Take turns pulling hips down toward the floor.

NOTES

This pose is not a tug-of-war, but a cooperative stretch-and-balance exercise.

PINWHEEL BREATH

BENEFITS

Calms and focuses. Uses breath awareness to sustain attention as activities change and tasks increase in difficulty. Regulates breathing and oxygenates the body. Good before a test or when students are upset or anxious.

TIME

3 to 20 minutes

ACTIVITY

- Practice Belly Breathing with Hoberman Sphere (p. 63), inhaling and exhaling slowly.

- Now, with a pinwheel in your hand, purse lips as if whistling and blow out to spin the pinwheel.

- See how slowly you can spin the pinwheel but without gasping for your next breath.

- To help slow your inhalation, imagine that you have another pinwheel in the back of your throat. Breathe in through the nose and make this imaginary pinwheel spin as slowly as possible too. Inhale and spin the inner pinwheel, exhale and spin the outer pinwheel.

- Set down the pinwheel, close your eyes and mouth, and breathe through the nose entirely. Imagine slowly spinning your inner and outer pinwheels with your breath.

VARIATIONS & INTEGRATION

- Keep the pinwheel continuously spinning for 10 seconds, then lengthen the time.

- Try Pinwheel Breath while in the Tree pose (p. 91).

- Spin the pinwheels to the beat of slow, steady music.

- Walk around the room to the beat of some slow music while spinning the pinwheels. Now, tap your leg with your hand to the beat of the music as you walk and spin the pinwheel at the same time!

- Find a partner and pat your free hands together (like patty-cake) to the beat of the music, while spinning the pinwheel. What did you experience doing this activity?

- Lead discussion on how to stay focused during challenging times, or read a story demonstrating what long-term, focused action can create such as Jean Giono's, *The Man Who Planted Trees*.

- Include pinwheels, windmills, water wheels, and so on in a Guided Relaxation (chapter 7).

NOTES

The pursed-lip breathing technique is one of the simplest ways to control shortness of breath and is often taught to asthmatics. It provides a quick and easy way to slow the pace of breathing, making each breath more effective and increasing oxygen to the brain.

PLANK

BENEFITS

Strengthens abdominal muscles, arms, and legs. Develops discipline, perseverance, and stamina. Great for developing a strong core—which is important for a strong life!

TIME

3 seconds to 2 minutes

ACTIVITY

- Come to all fours, with knees several inches behind hips.
- Point fingers straight ahead and spread them like rays of the sun.
- Press down through the four corners of each hand.
- Straighten one leg back, turn toes under, and place foot on floor. Do the same with the other leg and come into a push-up position with shoulders directly over or slightly behind the wrists.
- Lift legs, hips, belly, and head until body is straight like a board. Tailbone is kept tucked toward the floor.
- Press out through heels and top of head.
- Keep breathing!
- To avoid sagging at the hips and belly, breathe into your low back and imagine it lifting up to the sky like a balloon.

VARIATIONS & INTEGRATION

- Stretch a string out straight and line up ankle, knee, hip, shoulder, and ear.
- Lift low back up into a partner's hand.
- Develop more core strength by pulling the legs isometrically toward each other—using a yoga block between thighs to help—and pressing out through head and heels.
- Alternately lift one leg and then the other off the floor. Hug your lifting leg toward the midline to help.
- Alternate going from Plank to Downward Dog (p. 74) and back, keeping the belly and thighs up.
- Elbow Plank: Try Plank with elbows and palms on floor. Dolphin (p. 73) is a similar strength builder.
- Side Plank: From Plank, pull legs together, roll to outer edge of right foot while lifting the left arm up to the sky. Keep toes pulled back, lift hips, and lift heart to the sky. Repeat on other side.

PULSE COUNT

BENEFITS

Quiets and calms. Develops inner listening and personal awareness. Educates about the heart and circulatory system. Teaches about bodily rhythms and cycles of nature. Develops awareness that we do have control over our bodies.

TIME

2 to 20 minutes

ACTIVITY

- Take two fingers to the side of the mouth.
- Tip head slightly back and draw a line down with fingers into groove along the neck.
- Press gently to find pulse.
- Raise other hand when pulse is found.
- Count pulse beats silently to self.
- Now, count the pulse for 15 seconds. Later, expand to 30 seconds, and then 1 minute.
- Ask students what their count was. (*Note: Counts will vary and some students may have trouble counting or may make up exceptionally low or high counts.*)

VARIATIONS & INTEGRATION

- Run in place for one minute, then take pulse again. Discuss the reasons the pulse is different after running. Then try the opposite. Relax the muscles, slow the breathing, and concentrate on "thinking" your heart rate lower. Try playing relaxing music. What happens to the pulse?
- Time the group for 30 seconds, then have them do the math to calculate their pulse rate per minute.
- Older students can track their pulse and daily activities. Graph results, determine averages, and explore the relationships between activities and pulse.
- Take the pulse when students come in from recess and again after a 5-minute relaxation.
- Take the pulse when students are watching television, playing video games, and so on.
- Use as an introduction to a health lesson on the heart or stress. Include information on healthy resting and active heart rates.
- Show physical education charts for healthy aerobic heart training rates. Calculate each student's optimal training heart rate for their age.

NOTES

Pulse Count and breath awareness are simple biofeedback tools for determining healthy activities and for training the sympathetic nervous system to be less reactive to stressors. Athletes use pulse and breathing rate information to set their workout difficulty levels, and to gauge their condition and recovery rates.

An 8- to 10-year-old child's resting pulse rate is usually about 90 beats per minute, with rates varying from 60 to 110. Resting pulse rates much above 120 or much below 50 are uncommon and should be checked by a doctor (Lawrence Hall of Science, Family Health Program, 2001). Children's maximal heart rate is much higher than adults, and is generally 200 to 205 contractions per minute (Riner & Sabath, 2003).

ROCK AND ROLL

BENEFITS

Tones the spinal muscles, provides deep proprioceptive input, and stimulates the vestibular system, which supports physical balance and behavioral stability. Warms the body quickly. Develops abdominal/core strength. Massages back muscles.

TIME

30 seconds to 1 minute

ACTIVITY

- Place a yoga mat on floor or use another padded surface.
- Lie on back, bend knees toward chest, and grab shins.
- Slowly alternate rocking forward and back on the spine from hips to upper back.
- Press your belly down toward the floor as you roll up and down the spine.
- Go slowly enough that you maintain control and can feel each vertebra of the backbone pressing down toward the floor as you roll.
- Now, while still holding the knees, rock gently from side to side.

VARIATIONS & INTEGRATION

- Use this activity to prepare for Boat (p. 65): Without touching your feet to the floor, roll up to sitting bones and balance.
- Circles: Take knees out to the sides as you roll in a circle on your back. Imagine hugging a huge beach ball as you roll.
- As a calming activity, grasp knees and move them in small circles. This massages the low back, hips, and sacrum and stimulates a relaxation response.
- Use in lesson plan on anatomy and the skeletal system.

NOTES

Children with decreased discrimination of vestibular and proprioceptive information often exhibit poor posture, frequent falling, clumsiness, poor balance, constant moving and fidgeting, and poor attention. Treatment options like rolling provide vestibular and proprioceptive information and improve postural responses.

Using a yoga mat or padding and going slowly are important in this exercise to protect the bones of the back.

ROOTS

BENEFITS

Grounds, calms, and centers students. Strengthens ankles, feet, and postural muscles. Develops balance, personal awareness, and a sense of competence. Excellent activity for focusing students before a lesson.

TIME

1 to 2 minutes

ACTIVITY

- Stand with feet hip-width apart and pointing straight ahead (Mountain, p. 79).
- Rock forward and back with body Activated (firm and straight) and feet firmly on the floor.
- Make the rocking movement smaller and smaller until you balance on the center of your feet.
- Now rock side to side and then slowly return to center.
- Begin making big circles to the right. Notice how your weight shifts to the four edges of each foot as you circle. Notice how the foot muscles work to keep you upright.
- Make the circles smaller and smaller until you again come back to center.
- Make big circles to the left now. Then make circles smaller until back at center.

VARIATIONS & INTEGRATION

- Try the same activity with eyes closed.
- Invite students who snowboard, ski, or skateboard to share what they know about using the muscles in their feet to do these sports.
- Ask students to think about what it is that they are circling around, then share their responses.
- Use as a precursor to class lesson on gravity.
- Ask students to discuss what it means to be "centered."

NOTES

Roots is a terrific activity for teaching the alignment principle of grounding the four corners of the feet (p. 56) and is good preparation for teaching Mountain (p. 79) and standing balance poses such as Tree (p. 91) and Dancer (p. 72).

85

SHOULDER CLOCK

BENEFITS

Energizes and grounds. Develops cooperation and sensitivity. Stretches upper chest, shoulders, and arm muscles.

TIME

4 minutes

ACTIVITY

- Pair students by height and have them stand side by side, about 2 feet apart.
- Lift inside arms straight up and place palms together in twelve o'clock position.
- Breathe into upper chest and spread fingers.
- Exhale and take arms back about a foot to one o'clock position. Keep chest and top of head lifting.
- Repeat breath cycle and clocking of the arms until they are down by your sides at six o'clock.
- Switch sides.

VARIATIONS & INTEGRATION

- Use activity to teach young students the positions of the clock.

NOTES

This sequence is a good antidote for poor posture and the associated neck and shoulder fatigue that result from prolonged sitting, writing, and computer work with shoulders slumped.

SIDE ANGLE

BENEFITS

Energizes and grounds. Strengthens legs and core muscles. Stretches inner thighs and hip muscles. Excellent antidote for sitting too long.

TIME

10 seconds to 1 minute

ACTIVITY

- From standing, take legs wide apart—about 3 to 4 feet.
- Turn the left foot in slightly to the right, and the right foot all the way out to the right.
- Bend the right knee until thigh and calf form a right angle (knee over the ankle with shin straight up and down) and then lightly rest right elbow on right knee.
- Straighten the back leg and press out through feet and top of head.
- Stretch the left arm out over the left ear, palm facing down.
- Keep the head in alignment with the spine, with belly, chest, and eyes turned upward to the sky.
- Switch sides.

VARIATIONS & INTEGRATION

- Take hand from knee down to the floor by the little toe.
- Press gently on crown of head and have student "press back" in pose to engage more postural muscles.

NOTES

Pose stretches and tones the hip flexor and psoas, key muscles for posture and low back health.

STAR

BENEFITS

Energizes. Strengthens arms and legs. Develops a sense of center, balance, and personal power. Teaches the basic yoga alignment principles of Activating and Expanding (p. 54).

TIME

30 seconds to 1 minute

ACTIVITY

- From standing, take feet wide apart—about 3 to 4 feet—and point toes straight ahead.
- Take arms out to the sides and parallel to the floor.
- Activate (firm) muscles and extend out through arms, legs, head, and tail.
- Spread fingers like rays of the sun.

VARIATIONS & INTEGRATION

- Use the imagery of the sun or a star radiating outward.
- Have students think of something they would like to share with the world and shine it out like the sun.
- Create a "Galaxy" by having students come into a circle and press hands together while in each is in Star. Then move into Tree Circle (p. 93), while keeping hands together for support.

SUPERMAN

BENEFITS

Energizes. Strengthens the abdominals, back, shoulders, neck, and deep postural muscles. Activates and integrates both hemispheres of the brain.

TIME

30 seconds to 1 minute

ACTIVITY

- Lie on your belly with arms stretched out in front of you, thumbs pointing up.
- Lengthen and lift your right leg.
- Now lift your left arm, chest, and head.
- Look slightly down, and lengthen from top of head to tail.
- Switch sides and lift left leg and right arm.
- Now lift both arms and legs, the head, and the chest away from the floor.
- Reach out strongly through your arms and legs.
- Lengthen top of head and tail away from each other.
- Take a few deep breaths, then repeat once or twice more.

VARIATIONS & INTEGRATION

- Lift opposite arm and leg in unison for greater integration of brain hemispheres.
- In pose, lean to left and then right, like Superman banking a turn.
- Take arms out to the side like airplane wings, or alongside the body.

NOTES

Because most mental processes involve both sides of the brain, integration problems between the two hemispheres can result in inefficiencies in brain processes. Thus, some children with reading difficulties, central auditory processing disorders, language delay, and other learning problems may be suffering from such lack of hemispheric integration. This activity activates and integrates both hemispheres of the brain. Research indicates that this integration is related to ease of learning to read for school-age children.

This activity also can help with underdeveloped postural (extensor) muscles that can result from the amount of time children and babies spend sitting and on their backs.

See also Alternate Arm/Leg Kicks (p. 59) and Cobra (p. 71).

TABLE

BENEFITS

Energizes. Strengthens the back body (hamstrings, gluteals, shoulder blade muscles) and arms. Stretches the front body. Good for posture and grounding.

TIME

20 seconds to 1 minute

ACTIVITY

- Sit up on floor with feet flat on floor, close to hips, hip-width apart, toes pointing straight ahead. Hands are flat on the floor, behind the hips a few feet, with fingers pointing away from the body.
- Breathe in, press down through hands and feet, and lift heart and hips up until the front body is parallel with the floor.
- Top of head extends away from knees so that top of body is flat like a table.
- Knees stay bent at about a 90-degree angle.
- Hold pose for two to three breaths.
- To come down, keep chest lifting and lower hips back to ground.
- Do pose three times in a row.

VARIATIONS & INTEGRATION

- Drawbridge imagery: Inhale as you lift the bridge up. As you hold the pose and continue to breathe, let imaginary boats go under the bridge. Exhale as you lower the bridge.
- Hold a yoga block between the knees to develop more core strength and to keep knees from splaying out to the sides.
- Extend one leg out straight and parallel to floor. Supporting foot should be flat on the floor.
- Repeat with the other leg.

NOTES

Keep knees over ankles and all four corners of the foot on the ground (particularly the inner foot). Practice drawing the four corners of the foot before doing pose (p. 56).

To prepare for Table, use Bridge (p. 67).

Table pose strengthens and warms up hamstring muscles, preparing them for stretching as in Leg Extensions (p. 77). It can help also with underdeveloped postural (extensor) muscles that result from the amount of time children and babies spend sitting and on their backs.

TREE

BENEFITS

Energizes and calms. Develops balance and focuses attention. Strengthens postural muscles. Good for students with attention difficulties as it demands their immediate attention.

TIME

30 seconds to 2 minutes

ACTIVITY

- Stand with legs and feet together.
- Shift your weight onto the left foot.
- Slowly bend right knee and draw the right foot up, placing the sole as high as possible on the inner leg (i.e., ankle, shin, or thigh) without strain.
- Activate your body and press standing leg down, rooting yourself like a tree to the earth. Press palms together in front of heart to help with balance.
- Then, stretch arms and head up like branches to the sky, while rooting your standing leg.
- Repeat on the other leg.

VARIATIONS & INTEGRATION

- Dancing Trees: While in the pose, take the right arm back and the left arm forward, then switch, taking the left arm back and right forward.
- Try the pose with your eyes closed!
- Time students, lengthening holding times as the students grow stronger.
- Imagine a loved one holding the standing leg down to the ground.
- Have a few students who are good at the pose demonstrate. Have the class focus for them and then ask them what they think the demonstrators used to keep their balance. Write their strategies up on the board.

NOTES

Balance stimulation activities like Tree develop both vestibular and proprioceptive systems, which play a key role in perception, spatial awareness, and the development of motor, tactile, auditory, and visual brain systems. These activities are foundational to efficient brain processing and both academic and athletic performance. Additionally, balance treatment ameliorates anxiety and increases self-esteem in children with balance disorders.

Neurological screening tests indicate that 90 percent of children by age 5 to 6 should be able to balance on one foot for 10 seconds (Mutti, Martin, Sterling,et al, 1998).

To prepare for Tree, use Roots (p. 85), Tree Circle (p. 93), or just balance on one foot at a time. For trouble balancing, place one foot on top of the other, or try the pose with the back against a wall for support.

TREE CHALLENGE

BENEFITS

Develops grounding, focus, balance, trust, and teamwork in a fun way. Teaches how to keep centered when challenged.

TIME

2 to 5 minutes

ACTIVITY

TREE CHALLENGE I

- Have two students stand and face each other, one standing in Tree (p. 91) and the other challenging the balance of the one in the pose by jumping up and down, waving at them, and so on.
- Touching or blowing on the student in the pose is not allowed.
- Switch standing leg, repeat, and then partners switch roles.

TREE CHALLENGE II

- Students stand and face each other with their right legs up in Tree (p. 91), their right hands touching, and their left hands on their hips.
- At first, press hands gently toward each other for support. Then slowly begin to challenge each other by gently pressing back and forth, out to the sides, and so on without falling off balance.
- Don't grab or pull the other person's hand or push your hand into your partner's body.
- Switch arms, then switch legs.

VARIATIONS & INTEGRATION

- Ask students what helped them. (Typical responses include "I ignored the other person," "I said to myself, 'I am strong,'" and "I closed my eyes.") Use these in a group discussion as examples of how to stay centered when others are challenging or harassing. Write down the students' positive self-talk examples and strategies. Repeat the activity, having students try various strategies and positive self-talk.

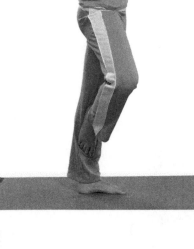

- Combine with Strong Voice activity (p.122).
- In Tree Challenge II, try to maintain eye contact.
- Imagine a loved one holding the standing leg down to the ground. Have students practice this game again with the support of that person.
- For a progressively harder balance sequence, start with Roots (p. 85) before moving to Tree (p. 91), Tree Circle (p. 93), and finally Tree Challenge.

NOTES

Challenging each other to be our best is one aspect of community support. This requires mutual trust and respect. This is a more advanced process to be used after students have developed some success with balancing as well as self-control, trust with each other, and a sense of community.

TREE CIRCLE

BENEFITS

Develops balance, trust, and teamwork in a fun way. Teaches how to stay centered when challenged.

TIME

2 to 5 minutes

ACTIVITY

- Students make a large circle, facing in and standing about 3 feet apart.
- Raise both arms and stretch them out, fingers pointing up.
- Place hands together with the person on each side and lift right leg up in Tree pose.
- Press into each other's hands and use each other for support.
- Switch legs and repeat.

VARIATIONS & INTEGRATION

- Have several of the students come out of the circle to be "animals" in the forest. Then re-form the circle and have the animals challenge the others by making noises, running in and out of the circle, jumping up and down, and so on (but no touching or blowing on the others). Switch challengers.
- Drop hands and try again without the support of the circle.
- Great sequence: Star Pose/Galaxy variation (p. 88), then Tree Circle, then add animal challengers, then animal challengers without the circle.

NOTES

In a forest, stands of trees shield each other from the wind, and intertwine their roots for greater support. Trees also provide habitat for animals. These and other themes can be developed from and explored through Tree Circle.

TRIANGLE

BENEFITS

Energizes and grounds. Strengthens legs and core muscles.

TIME

30 seconds to 1 minute

ACTIVITY

- Stand with legs wide apart—about 3 to 4 feet.
- Activate and straighten arms and legs.
- Turn your left foot in slightly to the right and your right foot all the way out to the right.
- Lift arms up and parallel to the floor.
- Now, shift upper body to right and "windmill" your arms over, taking the right hand to the shin, ankle, or yoga block.
- Stretch your left arm toward the ceiling.
- Press out through your legs, arms, and top of head (like Star, p. 88).

VARIATIONS & INTEGRATION

- Use Star (p. 88) as preparation.
- Use to teach basic geometry lesson (pose forms two triangles).

TWIST

BENEFITS

Grounds, energizes, and calms. Balances the nervous system. Improves digestion and organ tone.

TIME

10 to 20 seconds each side

ACTIVITY

CHAIR TWIST

- Sit in a chair with feet on the floor, hip-width apart.
- Press down through feet and sitting bones, and stretch up through top of head.
- Take left hand across the right knee and place right hand on the back of the chair.
- Slowly and gently turn belly, heart, and head toward the back of the chair.
- Inhale and lengthen the spine; exhale and twist.
- Shoulders stay back and down.
- Repeat on the other side.

FLOOR TWIST

- Lie on back.
- Pull knees up toward the chest, then over to the right and all the way to the floor.
- Stretch arms out to the sides and look to the left.
- Stretch your breath out to your fingertips.
- Bring knees back to center.
- Repeat on left side.

VARIATIONS & INTEGRATION

- Practice Belly Breathing (p. 63) while in the pose.
- Use with Calm Voice process (p. 106).

NOTES

Twists massage the abdominal organs, help with digestion, and maintain the normal length and resilience of the soft tissues. They also help to maintain the health of the vertebral discs and facet joints.

Twists can be used before or after any yoga sequence as a warm-up or cool-down. They are particularly effective as a transition to a relaxation or storytelling process.

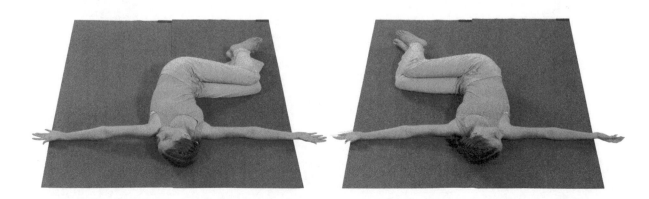

UPWARD MOUNTAIN AND CRESCENT MOON

BENEFITS

Grounds and energizes. Stretches and strengthens shoulders. Opens side ribs for a fuller breath. Wakes students up. Good after long periods of sitting and in preparation for testing.

TIME

1 to 2 minutes

ACTIVITY

UPWARD MOUNTAIN

- Stand with feet hip-width apart and arms straight up overhead.
- Palms face each other and fingers extend up.
- Press feet down and lift belly, head, and heart; shoulders back and down.
- Looks like football touchdown!

CRESCENT MOON

- From Upward Mountain, breathe in, press feet down, and stretch to the right slightly, curving into the shape of a crescent moon.
- Lengthen both sides of body.
- On an exhale, come back to center.
- Now stretch into Crescent Moon to the left.

VARIATIONS & INTEGRATION

- Imagine sending laser beams out through your fingertips.
- As you reach up to the sky, imagine sending energy from the center of the earth to the sun.

NOTES

Upward Mountain and Crescent Moon teach the basic alignment principles of Activating, Expanding, and pressing out through the four corners of the feet (p. 56). They are also excellent preparation for Tree (p. 91) and other standing balance poses.

VOLCANO BREATH

BENEFITS

Calms and centers. Develops inner imagery. Develops group movement and awareness. Releases tension, regulates breath, and develops compassion and sensitivity.

TIME

2 to 5 minutes

ACTIVITY

- Stand with feet hip-width apart, or sit in a chair or cross-legged on the floor.
- Place palms together at the heart.
- Take a slow, deep breath through the nose and pause when the lungs are full.
- Hold the pause and bring the arms up over the head.
- Exhale and slowly "explode the volcano," moving arms out to the side and then back together at heart.

VARIATIONS & INTEGRATION

- Think of someone or something you would like to send your heart thoughts to. Get the image of that person, animal, or place strongly in mind. On the next Volcano Breath, send your thoughts out to that person. Allow students to share who they sent their thoughts to.
- Ask students to think of something they would like to bring into their life. As they exhale, they can shower this image around them.
- Use stories of children sending positive thoughts to one another.

NOTES

Volcano breath with "heart thoughts" can also help to access and release underlying emotions that might inhibit the learning process (see p. 141).

WARRIOR I

BENEFITS

Energizes and grounds. Quickly warms the body. Develops strength, endurance, and flexibility. Good confidence builder before a test or a major challenge.

TIME

6 seconds to 1 minute

ACTIVITY

- Stand with legs hip-width apart.
- Take right leg back, placing the knee on floor (bent-knee version), or take right foot back 3 to 4 feet with heel off floor and straighten back leg (straight-leg version).
- Move hips forward and slide the back leg back until the front knee is right over the front ankle.
- Take arms overhead, palms facing each other and fingers extending.
- Lift belly, head, and heart.
- Repeat on other side.

(If the knee is uncomfortable in bent-knee version, double up mat or place padding under it.)

VARIATIONS & INTEGRATION

- Combine Warrior I pose with Strong Voice activity (p. 122).
- Have students pair up and face each other so they can see each other's strength.
- As students gain strength, increase the holding time.
- Useful cue: "Send lasers from your belly out through your fingers."

NOTES

The Warrior is a common archetype in many cultures, signifying the passage to adulthood, the protection of family and culture, and the ability to stand up for what one believes.

WARRIOR II

BENEFITS

Energizes and grounds. Develops leg and arm strength. Increases stamina.

TIME

1 to 2 minutes

ACTIVITY

- Stand with legs wide apart—about 3 to 4 feet.
- Turn your left foot in slightly to the right and your right foot all the way out to the right.
- Breathe in and lift arms up parallel to the floor, palms facing down.
- Exhale and bend the right knee until it is right over the ankle, with the shin straight up and down.
- Keep both sides of the torso equally long, with shoulders directly over the pelvis (there is a tendency to lean to the bent-knee side).
- Shoulders are back and down.
- Extend out through top of head, tail, feet, and arms.
- Repeat on other side.

(p. 56)

VARIATIONS & INTEGRATION

- Use Star (p. 88) as preparation, noting its arm and torso position.
- In the pose, work on widening the stance until front thigh is parallel with the floor, with knee over the ankle. Quite a workout!
- Rising Moon: Reach your front palm up to the sky and take the back hand to the back thigh.
- In your heart, think of the people you care about and then extend your heart thoughts out to them.
- This pose is also used in the Past, Present, and Future activity (p. 119).

WOODCHOPPER

BENEFITS

Releases tension. Energizes and stimulates the nervous system. Develops focus and strengthens breathing (diaphragm) muscles. Combined with use of voice, helps students find their personal power.

TIME

1 to 2 minutes

ACTIVITY

- Stand with feet a little wider than hip-width apart and knees slightly bent.
- Take arms overhead with hands together as if holding an ax.
- Imagine a piece of wood on the ground in front of you.
- On a count of three, swing hands down to chop the imaginary piece of wood.
- Make a loud "Huh!" sound as your ax hits the imaginary wood.

VARIATIONS & INTEGRATION

- Make the "Huh" sound come from the deepest part of the belly. Ask if students feel a difference doing it this way.
- When students picture the piece of wood on the floor in front of them, encourage them to really keep their focus on the wood as they chop down so they don't miss it.
- Have individual students lead the pose in front of the classroom.
- Ask students to Activate (p. 54) their body before the activity and observe the difference.
- Combine with Pulse Count activity (p. 83) before and after to check the effect of the pose.
- Combine with Strong Voice activity (p. 122) to develop students' personal power.
- Use before a test to make students more alert and/or to reduce anxiety and tension.

NOTES

Exercise empties lungs completely, creating a slight vacuum that pulls in fresh air.

Use before a test to increase alertness and reduce anxiety and tension.

Yoga Calm Tools 6
Social/Emotional Activities

Teaching Social/Emotional Skills

At a social gathering we recently attended, Tony, a 45-year-old man with a wife and family, was discussing the importance of teaching social and emotional skills. As a teenager, Tony had been so painfully shy that he had difficulty making friends, dating girls, or succeeding in job interviews. Since both of his parents were also extremely shy, they could not guide him in this area.

Being an intelligent and observant man, Tony eventually decided that he needed to learn about communication and social etiquette. He went to the library, checked out several books on emotions, social development, and communication, and taught himself the skills he had lacked. This self-education changed his life. As he began to practice the new skills, he became more confident and successful in his social interactions. He began to ask open-ended questions, reflect feelings, and show interest in others. He remarked how "teachable" these skills were and expressed concern for children and adults who struggle with poor skills yet have no idea that it's not a personal flaw but a lack of education that interferes with their success in life.

> *I had been invited to give a lesson on friendship skills to a second-grade class. The students sat in a circle on the rug, and I asked two students to come into the center. I set out a basket of puppets and a basket of blocks. The students practiced inviting one another to play, then negotiating whether they wanted to play with the blocks or the puppets.*
>
> *I asked the class if it was ever OK to say no when another student invites you to play. They shook their heads to say no, then nodded yes, then wagged no again. They'd been taught to be kind and polite. But how to set limits while also being compassionate? This was their obvious struggle.*
>
> *So we practiced saying no politely. Through role-playing, we said things like "I feel like playing alone today, but I would like to play with you another time." And, "I'm in the middle of something right now, but maybe later." We talked about the need to be alone at times and ways to say no while still letting others know that we care about them.*
>
> *After the lesson the teacher said, "I wish someone had taught me that as a child. I still have trouble saying no, and I make promises I am not able to keep."*

As such stories demonstrate, social and emotional skills are crucial to success and happiness in life. People without these skills have a difficult time caring for themselves and finding meaningful relationships. Also, it has been found that when students receive training in social/emotional learning (SEL), their test scores improve and they are less likely to drop out of school.

An SEL program developed in Hudson, Massachusetts, is now taught to all students there. The results have been significant. Sheldon Berman, Hudson School District superintendent, reports that since the SEL curriculum was introduced, both attendance and student dropout rates have improved significantly. In addition, SAT scores and fourth- and sixth-grade achievement scores have risen, and the number of students enrolled in Advanced Placement courses has tripled.

" … studies of [SEL] programs showed that students … academic achievement tests were a hefty 12 percent higher …"

What makes Hudson's SEL program different from other character education programs is that it is skill-based. That is, it breaks down the skills necessary to thrive socially and emotionally, and teaches these skills to the students. This is in contrast to the many character education programs that rely largely on lectures and rote learning. Just as children need to practice reading, writing, and math skills on a regular basis, they also must practice social and emotional skills. And just as it would be unreasonable to lecture students about the importance of math yet never give them practice drills, so, too, with social/emotional learning.

Children must be shown how to recognize and process emotions, learning how to respond appropriately. Taking the time to listen and guide children through conflict when it arises helps them to gain understanding and tolerance of others—just two of the qualities children can learn through practice, along with compassion, empathy, self-awareness, and many other complementary qualities.

> *Fourth-graders Jamie and Juan requested a meeting in my room. Juan was angry because, out on the playground, Jamie had called him a swear word. Now he was shut down. His arms were crossed, and he glared at Jamie.*
>
> *I asked Jamie to tell me his side of the story, and he began to cry. He said that the students on the playground would not let him join in the games. He said that Juan had been one of his best friends, and even he wouldn't let Jamie play. With tears running down his face, he told Juan, "I thought you would let me play. I thought I could count on you."*
>
> *Seeing Jamie's emotion opened Juan's heart, and he began to soften. He said that he was his friend, but that they were already involved in their game; it was too late to have another person join.*
>
> *The boys spent several minutes talking it out. They apologized to each other and agreed to play together during the next recess.*

Although it is time-consuming to provide opportunities for children to process emotions, the results can have far-reaching effects not only in their social success, but also in their ability to focus on academics. In his groundbreaking book *Emotional Intelligence*, Daniel Goleman writes that of the "dozens of programs" for teaching social/emotional skills, "the best are designed to fit into the standard school curriculum for children at every age and include skills like self-awareness and managing distressing emotions, empathy and navigating relationships smoothly. A definitive meta-analysis of more than one hundred studies of these programs showed that students not only mastered abilities like calming down and getting along better, but, more to the point here, learned more effectively: their grades improved—and their scores on academic achievement tests were a hefty 12 percent higher than similar students who did not have the programs."

The activities in this chapter are designed to teach children these crucial social and emotional skills. They give children opportunities to practice empathy, trust, and compassion, and to develop a strong sense of community. We encourage teachers and counselors to integrate these games into their curriculum and regular yoga classes for children. If during these activities, emotions arise, use the tools listed in chapter 8 and refer to the school counselor when necessary. It has been our experience that if emotions are addressed regularly in the classroom, outbursts are reduced and children feel safe and supported.

ARCHETYPE GAME

BENEFITS

Energizes. Helps students discriminate between different roles and when to use them in life. Develops personal awareness.

TIME

15 to 20 minutes

ACTIVITY

Students spread out around the room, each in a squatting position.

Then, on a slow count to 4, they grow into a statue that represents a specific archetype or character, such as a king or queen. (See list below.) Then, with music playing, ask the students to move the way their archetype or character would move. When you say "Freeze," all students stop and squat again. Start over with a different archetype.

Students must give each other space when they come to a squatting position. No touching, running, or talking is allowed. Any student who breaks the rules must sit out for one archetype before rejoining the game.

VARIATIONS & INTEGRATION

Before the students start, ask them to pay attention to which archetypes are easy or natural for them and which are uncomfortable to act out. After playing, ask students to share which characters were their favorites. Ask them to brainstorm when we need to use each archetype and when a particular one might be dangerous (e.g., Kind and Friendly when around strangers) or get them in trouble (e.g., The Trickster when company comes over for dinner).

Allow students to be the archetypes or characters in a novel or story, or have them share the parts of themselves they use in football, dancing, snowboarding, or other favorite activities.

See illustrative story on page 145.

Some Archetypes

- The Trickster—the sneaky self
- The Warrior—the fierce one
- Prince or Princess—connecting with our sense of pride and elegance
- Wise King or Queen—stepping into responsibility
- Monster—our scary self
- Angel—our kind and giving self
- The Content One—feeling satisfied with who we are and our own personal gifts
- Kind and Friendly One—our social self
- Bear or the Hermit in the Cave—taking time to be alone
- Peaceful One—the quiet, contemplative self
- Clown—our silly self
- Courageous Explorer—facing adversity

CALM VOICE

BENEFITS

Helps students develop a calm or peaceful voice that can be used during difficult experiences. Develops students' ability to self-soothe. Helps them remember who in their life they go to for this quality.

TIME

10 to 15 minutes

ACTIVITY

Students sit in chairs or lie on the floor. Practice a breathing activity to help them ground and turn their awareness inside. It is helpful to play quiet music.

Slowly read the sentences to them on the Calm Voice Worksheet, opposite, pausing long enough for them to process the ideas that come into their minds. After reading, ask students to open their eyes and fill out the page. This should be done without talking. Allow students to share their responses.

VARIATIONS & INTEGRATION

Ask students to talk about people and places that help them feel calm.

As a homework assignment, ask students to read a relaxation story (see chapter 7) to a parent, friend, or sibling. Remind them that they will need to find their calm voice in order to do this.

NOTES

It is not uncommon for students to name God, Jesus, or other religious figures when they identify a voice of peace inside of them. When this occurs, allow the students to share their experience. As long as they don't tell others how to feel or what to believe, this is a wonderful opportunity for children to feel that they are able to have their personal spiritual beliefs at school—and it gives teachers and students a chance to practice acceptance.

CALM VOICE WORKSHEET

Where in your body do you find your calm voice?

_____

_____

Is the voice high or low?

_____

Does the voice talk fast or slow?

_____

When you hear your calm voice, who does it sound like?

_____

_____

What does it say?

_____

_____

Are there places you go where you can hear your calm voice?

_____

_____

When can a calm voice help you?

_____

_____

CHANGING CHANNELS

BENEFITS

Teaches students the skill of shifting their attention and gives practice with this skill. Develops imagination. Helps them to focus on positive and healthy thoughts.

TIME

1 to 5 minutes

ACTIVITY

Ask the students to shut their eyes and notice what they begin to think about—what is on their minds. Then tell them they are going to practice changing the channel in their minds.

Now ask them to change the channel by imagining themselves playing in the snow: "Imagine that you are all bundled up in a coat, hat, and mittens, and you are having a snowball fight with a friend." Keep them on that channel for 30 seconds or so, then have them change the channel to a sunny beach, imagining that they are lying on a towel with the sun shining on their face. Again hold that image for 30 seconds, then change the channel. Do this four or five times, then ask a student to change the channel for the group. It may help to give ideas. A few are offered below.

Afterward, ask the students when this activity might be useful. (Typical answers include "when I'm worried," "when I have a nightmare," or "when I've seen a scary movie and I keep seeing the images over and over again.") Ask students how they might use this tool when they are about to take a test or do something challenging.

IDEAS FOR CHANNELS

- At home on the couch, drinking a warm cup of cocoa
- Baking a batch of cookies and smelling them in the oven
- Playing outdoors with a friend
- Swimming
- Being in a favorite place
- Holding a small pet
- Riding a bike
- Picking a bouquet of flowers
- Walking in the forest

VARIATIONS & INTEGRATION

Shift from something frightening to something pleasurable and notice the responses in the body.

Have the students walk around the room, shift attention, and notice whether it affects the pace of their walking.

Combine with Pinwheel Breath (p. 81), asking students to think of different things while they are breathing and notice the effects on the breath.

Combine with a balance pose and notice the effects of shifting attention on their ability to balance.

NOTES

As in relaxation activities (chapter 7), it is helpful to include sensory details (scents, sounds, sights, tastes, and physical sensations) when asking students to imagine.

COMMUNICATION GAME

BENEFITS

Teaches communication skills and gives students practice with these skills.

TIME

20 to 30 minutes

ACTIVITY

Draw the following chart on a blackboard, whiteboard, or large piece of paper. Write down the first situation and leave the dialogue boxes empty. Tell students they are going to learn some skills that will help them communicate more clearly with friends and relatives.

Ask the students to imagine that a friend comes up and remarks, "Joe won't let me join the kickball game." Then go through the different ways to respond, starting with Restate and ending with Encourage or Empathize, as in the example below. After showing the first two situations, ask the class to come up with responses for the last scenario.

SITUATION	RESTATE	REFLECT FEELINGS	ASK QUESTIONS	SHARE YOUR EXPERIENCE	ENCOURAGE OR EMPATHIZE
Joe won't let me join the kickball game.	He said you can't play?	You look mad. You sound frustrated.	When did he say that? Who was there? Did anyone stick up for you?	Tony did that to me on Tuesday.	That is so annoying!
Mary told Frank that I like him!	She told Frank?	You sound upset.	How do you know she told him? What did you say to her?	I've had girls do that to me. I was really mad.	I'm sorry she did that. I know you didn't want anyone to tell.
My mom won't let me go to the slumber party.					

After completing the third scenario, divide the class into two groups. Ask two volunteers from Group 1 to come to the front of the room. Write a new situation in the next row of the matrix and tell the students they will have three minutes to keep a conversation going using the different communication skills. Each time they use one of the skills, put a check under each skill. Each check is worth a point. If the two people get stuck, they can ask for help from others on their team. Then have two students from Group 2 do the same. The group with the most points at the end of the game wins.

It is best to go two or three rounds before declaring a winner so the students have more time to practice.

After playing this game in groups, have students divide into pairs and practice together for 2 to 3 minutes. It helps to give them a subject such as "Tell about a time when you were really scared."

COMMUNITY CIRCLE

BENEFITS

Helps students identify their community support. Especially helpful for students who have experienced a loss or who are going through a difficult time.

TIME

10 to 20 minutes

ACTIVITY

Ask students to close their eyes and think of the people in their community. Encourage them to think of those they see every day, and also those they see only once in a while. Ask them to think of the people who help them in their daily lives, such as teachers, bus drivers, mail carriers, store clerks, and so on. Then give students the Community Circle Worksheet, opposite. Ask the students to place themselves in the center and fill in the circles around them with the names of people in their community. The names they put in the inner circle are those the student sees often and is close to. Those in the outer circle are people in their community who may not be there on an everyday basis. Allow students to decorate and share their community circles with one another.

VARIATIONS & INTEGRATION

After reading a story or novel, identify the community support that helped the main character.

Read a story about community members, or make cards for the individuals in the school community (e.g., janitors, secretaries) to thank them for the work they do.

Create a class community circle with all the students in the center and people who help the class in the outer circles.

COMMUNITY
CIRCLE
WORKSHEET

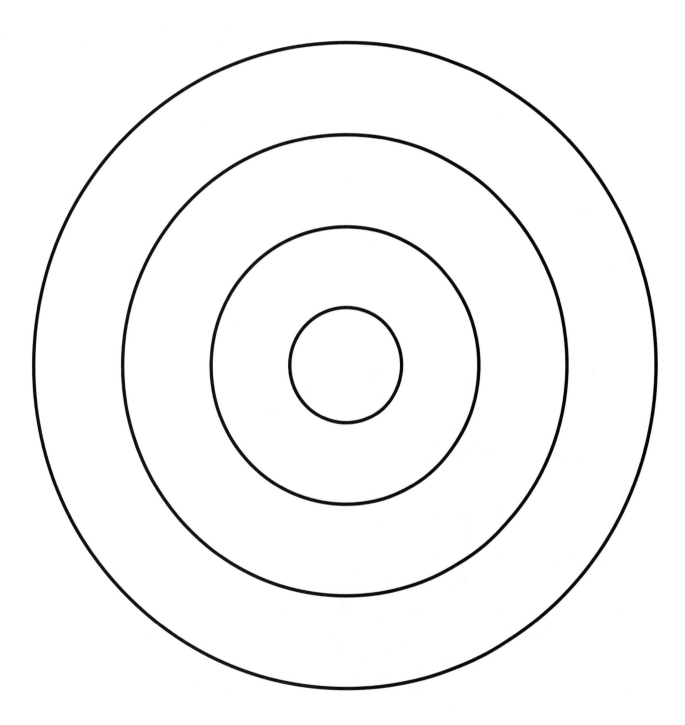

COMPLIMENT GAME

BENEFITS

Teaches students how to give and receive compliments. Great for building self-esteem, compassion, and community among students.

TIME

5 to 30 minutes, depending on number of students

ACTIVITY

Students all form a large circle by grasping a large Hoberman Sphere or holding a rope loop or two yoga straps connected together. Ask one student to come into the circle's center and the others to take turns giving the student a compliment. Have the students practice making eye contact with the student in the middle, saying their name, and giving specific compliments (e.g., "I really liked the way you helped me in Tree Pose today."). The student receiving the compliments should look back at the person and thank them for their words.

VARIATIONS & INTEGRATION

Put the teacher or a parent in the compliment sphere. It's a fun surprise, and the children love it!

Give compliments based on something particular, such as one thing the student does well or one thing that person has done for others.

NOTES

Holding the sphere, or a rope loop, helps students focus and gives them something to do with nervous energy.

BENEFITS

Helps students identify and evaluate different feelings and learn to make healthy choices. Develops compassion, understanding, and discernment.

TIME

30 to 40 minutes

ACTIVITY

Ask a student volunteer to come to the front of the room. Ask the class to imagine that it is a hot day in July and the student is standing on a steep cliff, looking into the cool river below. A friend of the student has encouraged him or her to jump into the water below. The student has two conflicting feelings that are speaking very loudly inside his or her body. What are they?

On a chalkboard, whiteboard, or piece of paper, write each of the two feelings the class identifies side by side. Ask the class what each word is saying to the student, then write those responses under each word. For instance, if the words are "afraid" and "brave," under the former, you might write things like, "You'll die!" or "You'll break a leg!" Under the latter, you might write, "Don't be a wimp!" or "You can do it!" Encourage the class to come up with seven or eight responses for each feeling.

Now ask for two students to play the parts of the different voices. Standing on either side of the person about to jump, have each student read their respective feelings from the board. After watching this for a few minutes, ask the class which voice they think the student should obey. Allow the student volunteers to sit down, and ask the group if it is possible for the student to listen to both feelings. Help them come to a solution that honors both feelings. For instance, some solutions to the face-off between feeling both afraid and brave could include jumping from a lower rock after checking the depth of the water; watching others jump and then deciding if it's safe; and asking others for information in order to make a better decision.

VARIATIONS & INTEGRATION

Try this activity presenting a situation that generates other feelings: anger and calm, responsibility and playfulness—any pair of feelings that people may struggle with when making a decision.

An important part of this activity is to help students learn that the feelings are not bad—they are warning systems from the body. It is helpful to ask students what life would be like if we only listened to fear, and what might happen if we only listened to our bravery—or any other single feeling that gets mentioned in the activity. In this way, students can learn how to listen to, evaluate, and balance competing thoughts and emotions.

CONFLICTING FEELINGS

EXPLORING FEELINGS

BENEFITS

Helps students learn to identify and express feelings, to understand the messages that feelings are sending, and to care for themselves.

TIME

15 to 40 minutes

ACTIVITY

Brainstorm a list of feelings with the class and write them on the board. Ask students the purpose of these different feelings and record their responses. Then ask students to come to the front of the class and act out one of the feelings listed on the board. Give the class three guesses. If the class hasn't guessed correctly after three tries, have the actor reveal the feeling.

Discuss with the students how different feelings can look the same—for instance, how it can be hard to tell the difference between loneliness and tiredness. Discuss with the class how to find out what a person is feeling—and the danger of assuming you know what someone else feels. Discuss posture and how this can communicate a feeling. Have students demonstrate a posture of strength and one of victimization.

VARIATIONS & INTEGRATION

Have students demonstrate two feelings at once in the body.

Have students demonstrate "hidden" feelings: putting on a feeling that covers a different one.

Have students act out a sudden change in feelings. How does this look? When does this happen?

Discuss ways to care for yourself when certain feelings emerge. What do you do to take care of loneliness? Or fear? Or some other feeling? This can be done as a class or in smaller groups.

Combine with a 1- to 5-minute silence to check in with the body to see what it is feeling in the present moment. Ask students to share what their bodies are feeling and to describe what they might need to do to take care of themselves because of those feelings.

BENEFITS

Helps students identify their personal paths to happiness. Also helps develop an understanding of individual differences.

TIME

20 to 30 minutes

ACTIVITY

Give students the Happiness Recipe Worksheet (p. 116). Ask them to complete the sentences on the sheet. This should be done without talking. It is helpful to do a breathing activity like Belly Breathing (p. 63) first to slow them down and direct their awareness inward. After they complete the sheet, ask students to share what they have written.

VARIATIONS & INTEGRATION

For a homework assignment, ask students to give the handout to their parents, siblings, or a friend and report back on what they learned.

Discuss how good it feels when a friend or family member knows you and plans a day with your interests and joys in mind—your favorite color on the cake, an offer to play your favorite game, and so on.

Since the activity sheet includes things like exercise, the class can discuss how important health is to happiness. When people are sick or in pain, it is hard to be happy, so caring for oneself is also an important aspect of happiness.

Use the activity to develop understanding of personal differences. Each student's recipe will be unique—yet there are commonalities too. You may want to point out that money and prestige are not what students most often identify as things that make them happy. Most common are friendship, time with family, and activities they love.

HAPPINESS RECIPE WORKSHEET

My favorite activities:

_____

An animal that is like me:

_____

An exercise I enjoy:

_____

How I spend time alone:

_____

How I spend time with others:

_____

Things that make me feel happy:

_____

My favorite memories:

_____

Things I do well:

_____

How do I ask for help when I need it:

_____

Other things that will make my life happy:

_____

BENEFITS

Gives children practice at standing up for themselves and protecting themselves from bullying behavior. Develops verbal and nonverbal communication skills.

TIME

10 to 20 minutes

ACTIVITY

Ask a volunteer to come to the front of the room and slowly chase you. Then, as the child is chasing you, laugh and tease and say "stop" in a playful way. Then ask the students why this didn't work very well. They know that it is because the person being chased was giving a double message. Write this on the board:

Double Message

1. My language said, "Stop."

2. My body language said, "Keep going, I'm having fun."

Ask the students which message they believe. Most will say they believe the body. Discuss with the class double messages that moms, dads, siblings, and friends sometimes send. Then go over the following steps for addressing harassment. After explaining the following steps, have two students at a time practice chasing each other (slowly) and demonstrate to the class the process of sticking up for oneself. Students love this activity.

STOPPING HARASSMENT

The steps:

1. In a kind way, tell the person to stop.

2. Say it again. This time, ground your feet, use your strong voice, and say the person's name.

3. Give a warning—for example, "I'm going to tell a teacher," or "I'm going to stop playing with you." (Brainstorm with children warnings they can give.)

4. Tell a teacher or follow through with the warning.

5. Make an appointment with the school counselor.

6. You may have to do this many times before a person will stop the harassing behavior. Keep trying, and believe in yourself.

VARIATIONS & INTEGRATION

Combine with Strong Voice (p. 122) or Woodchopper (p. 100) to help students find and communicate strength through their body and voice.

HARASSMENT PREVENTION

MINDFUL SNACK

BENEFITS

Calming. Develops good eating habits, manners, gratitude, and appreciation for beauty—and serves as remembrance that beauty and peace are available to us in the present moment. (One of the translations for mindfulness is remembrance.) Also a much calmer way to celebrate holidays and have class parties!

TIME

30 minutes

ACTIVITY

This beautiful activity requires some preparation. Begin by finding some colorful paper and coordinating decorative paper napkins. Turn down lights and put on soothing music. Give students antiseptic towelettes that they can use first to wash their hands, then to wipe the desk or table in front of them.

Pass the paper around so that each student has a piece to use for a placemat. Next pass a small basket of napkins and have each student take a napkin to spread out onto their placemat. Ask students to admire the artwork in the napkin. Then pass around a basket or bowl with the names of the students in it. The names can be beautifully handwritten or printed on small pieces of textured paper using a special font. Have each student find their name and place this on their mat. Pass a bowl or tray of cups and have the students each pick out a cup for their setting. (We use a collection of glasses, which we ask the students to treat carefully—as if they were kings and queens—but paper cups work, too.) Then pass around a bowl or basket of beautiful natural objects with which the students can decorate their placemats. You can use small flowers, leaves, rocks, pine cones—things from the natural world. Allow each student to pick two or three items.

When the mats have been decorated, pass around a bowl of fresh fruit and a small amount of chocolate or other dessert. Ask the students to take a portion of each and set the food on their placemat. Pass around a pitcher of fresh juice and have them pour a glass for themselves. No eating until everyone is served. Once everyone has been served, take a minute to tell them about the food they are about to eat: what kind of fruit it is, where it came from, the flavor of the juice, the type of chocolate. It can also be fun to think of all the things that occurred to bring the food to them—the people who grew it, the trucks that carried it, and so on.

Then enjoy the snack!

VARIATIONS & INTEGRATION

Try serving a local food that may not be something the children eat regularly. Have you had a persimmon? A star fruit?

Allow students to collect items from outdoors to decorate their placemat.

Combine activity with Community Circle (p. 110), identifying who provides them with food in their community.

BENEFITS

Connects students to their community support. Develops and strengthens personal awareness. Especially powerful for students who have lost loved ones. (Note: If any student needs extra support, schedule a private time for the student to meet with you or the counselor, or help the student identify someone else who will support him or her.)

TIME

10 to 15 minutes

ACTIVITY

Ask the students to come into Warrior II pose (p. 99). As they hold the pose, tell them that the back hand represents the past and the front hand represents the future. Then explain that we want to be aware of the past and the effects it has on us, and also aware of our future goals. Our eyes are looking in the direction of the future, but we keep our awareness of and respect for the past. We don't want to be stuck in the past, or too far into the future, so we keep our weight balanced in the middle—the present moment.

If students are working with a difficult past, acknowledge that difficulty in a general way and encourage them to think of how that difficulty has made them stronger human beings. When they have done this physical activity, ask them to fill out the Past, Present, and Future Worksheet (p. 120), then share their results.

VARIATIONS & INTEGRATION

Have the students think of a person who has been there for them in the past when things have been difficult. With that person in mind, allow the students to pick a small stone from a bowl of stones. While they hold Warrior II, they can hold the stone in their back hand as a reminder that they will always carry that person with them, inside them.

Read stories or give examples of people who have used past challenges and experiences to help others.

PAST, PRESENT, AND FUTURE

PAST, PRESENT, AND FUTURE WORKSHEET

FUTURE GOALS

THOSE WHO SUPPORT US

PERSONAL SPACE

BENEFITS

Helps students to identify their own personal space and to accept individual differences. Teaches the relationship between personal space and feeling states. Improves nonverbal communication skills.

TIME

10 to 30 minutes

ACTIVITY

Ask two volunteers to come to the front of the room. Have them stand about 10 to 12 feet apart, facing each other. Ask Student 1 to begin walking slowly toward Student 2. As Student 1 nears, Student 2 raises a hand to show the boundary of his or her personal space.

Now ask Student 2 to walk toward Student 1 and see if that person's personal boundary is the same or different.

Try it with several other students, noticing the difference in individuals' needs for personal space. During one turn, ask a student to walk right into the other person's space and ask the class to notice the nonverbal cues that the person being approached gives. The students may notice things like laughing, turning the face away, leaning way back, blushing, and so on.

Brainstorm a list of the things that can affect a person's need for personal space. The list might include things like how well the two know each other, personal hygiene, gender, how a person feels that day, height, family and culture, and profession or occupation.

VARIATIONS & INTEGRATION

Have students assemble in two lines, facing each other. Have one line walk toward the other until each student comes to the boundary of another's personal space. Notice the differences in people. Alter the lines and repeat.

STRONG VOICE

BENEFITS

Helps students identify their strength and discuss the ways they can use it to help them in their lives. Especially helpful for students who have lost touch with their sense of strength and those who have developed it in unhealthy ways.

TIME

10 to 15 minutes

ACTIVITY

Students sit in chairs or lie on the floor with their eyes closed. Practice a breathing activity to help them ground and turn their awareness inside. It is helpful to play quiet music.

Slowly read the sentences to them on the Strong Voice Worksheet, opposite, pausing long enough for them to process the ideas that come into their minds. After reading, ask students to open their eyes and fill out the page. This should be done without talking. Ask students to share their responses.

VARIATIONS & INTEGRATION

Combine this activity with a story of a warrior or young heroine.

Combine with the Archetype Game (p. 105), asking students to "be" their strong self.

Combine with the Harassment Prevention activity (p. 117).

Discuss how strength can be used when one is angry. Give role models such as Dr. Martin Luther King Jr., who used his anger and strength together for positive change.

Discuss how strength can be used in negative ways and how people can keep this from happening.

NOTES

Students often name a grandparent or parent who has died as the voice they hear when they listen for their strong voice. This activity can be an opportunity to learn how to keep that loved one close.

STRONG VOICE WORKSHEET

Can you find the strong voice inside of you?

_____

Where do you feel the strong voice in your body?

_____

Is the voice high or low?

_____

Is the voice loud or soft?

_____

Does the voice make you think of someone?

_____

What does the voice say?

_____

What can you do to find your strong voice when you are angry or afraid?

_____

When do you need your strong voice?

_____

Draw a picture of yourself feeling strong:

TRICKSTER

BENEFITS

Helps students identify the trickster in themselves and develop this aspect of the personality in ways that are useful or otherwise positive. Develops personal awareness. Especially helpful for children who tend to get in trouble and have thus developed a negative perception of the part of themselves that likes to be sneaky or playful.

TIME

10 to 15 minutes

ACTIVITY

Students sit in a chair or lie on the floor. Practice a breathing activity to help them ground and turn their awareness inside. It is helpful to play some "sneaky," suspenseful, or quiet music.

Slowly read the sentences to them on the Trickster Archetype Worksheet, opposite, pausing long enough for them to process the ideas that come into their minds. After reading, ask students to open their eyes and fill out the page. This should be done without talking. Ask students to share their responses.

VARIATIONS & INTEGRATION

Combine this activity with a story of Coyote, Crow, or another traditional trickster. These can be found in various collections of myths and legends.

Combine with the Archetype Game (p. 105), allowing students to "be" their trickster self.

TRICKSTER ARCHETYPE WORKSHEET

Think of a time it was fun to be sneaky.

How did you move?

_____

When is it helpful to be sneaky?

_____

When does it get you in trouble?

_____

How do you breathe when you are sneaking?

_____

Can you think of an animal that is sneaky?

_____

Are there times when being sneaky can keep you safe?

_____

Draw a picture of a time when it was fun to be sneaky:

TRUST WALK AND SENSORY ADVENTURE

BENEFITS

Develops trust, sensitivity, and personal awareness. Helps develop ability to read facial cues and nonverbal communication. Great for teambuilding and developing a sense of community. Develops tactile and other nonvisual senses.

TIME

15 to 25 minutes

ACTIVITY

TRUST WALK

Ask one volunteer to come to the front of the room. Have that student hold the index finger of one hand out as if about to ring a doorbell. Ask the student to shut his or her eyes. Then, with your index finger, hook onto the student's finger.

Now demonstrate the activity by carefully leading the student, still with their eyes closed, around the room. Demonstrate moving slowly and watching their feet and face for nonverbal cues as to whether they feel safe. Let the students know that their role as a guide is to make the person they are guiding feel safe. Demonstrate backing the student up, turning in different directions, and so on.

Then tell the group that everyone will have a "surprise" guide. Explain that half of the group will get up, find a place to stand in the room, close their eyes, and hold out their index fingers. The other half will quietly find a person to guide. It is important that the person guiding does not talk or laugh, because that would spoil the surprise at the end. Also mention that the students leading the activity will have to direct traffic in the room without talking. They will have to do this with a hand gesture or other body language. Demonstrate how this might look.

After the students have led one another around for 3 to 5 minutes, ask them to stop moving. Those being led should keep their eyes shut while they guess out loud who has been guiding them. Then they can open their eyes.

SENSORY ADVENTURE

After the Trust Walk, students will guide each other again. This time they take their friend—whose eyes are closed—to different objects in the room, gently place the person's hand on the object, and let them guess what they are touching. It can be fun to bring in interesting objects with various textures and shapes to place around the room (e.g., soft socks, rocks, statues, leaves). The students who are guiding remain silent to keep the surprise at the end of the game. The students being guided can say out loud what they think the object is, but guides do not respond.

VARIATIONS & INTEGRATION

Many lessons can be developed from this game. You can discuss friendship and the importance of leading and following. Students can share about who leads certain activities in their home and who leads others. It can be a good lesson on reading nonverbal cues and letting others know you are someone who can be trusted.

NOTES

We find it helpful to have some music in the background.

If students are not playing safely, ask them to watch and then join in on the next game.

YES/NO GAME

BENEFITS

Teaches the concepts of positive and negative reinforcement, and allows students to experience the benefits of positive reinforcement. Teaches communication skills, cooperation, and cultural awareness.

TIME

20 to 40 minutes

ACTIVITY

Ask one student to go out of the room. Have another student pick an object in the room that can be touched. Don't place the object too high or have it out of view. Then tell the class that when the student comes back into the room, you are going to help that person find the object by using negative reinforcement. (It is helpful to write the term on the board.)

Practice with the class before bringing the child back into the room. Stand in the center of the room and tell the students that as you go in the wrong direction, they are to quietly say "No," and when you go in the right direction, they are to say nothing. Practice until the students are able to do this without yelling or giving conflicting messages. Then bring the student back into the room and play the game until the student finds the object.

Then ask another student to leave the room, and pick a different object. This time the class will help the student find the object using positive reinforcement. Practice by placing yourself in the center and this time, when you move in the right direction, the students say "Yes," and when you go in the wrong direction, they say nothing. Play the game a second time using positive reinforcement.

Discuss with the students the benefits of these two kinds of reinforcement and when they work and when they don't. Give examples of using positive reinforcement in schools, businesses, at home, and elsewhere.

VARIATIONS & INTEGRATION

CULTURAL AWARENESS

Play the game again, asking one student to go out of the room. This time tell the class that they have landed on Mars and no longer speak English. Have a student in the class make up a word or sound for "No." Practice the game using negative reinforcement with the new word. Have the student come in and play the game. Ask the student to try to figure out what the word means. Play it again with a made-up word for "Yes," then again with two words: one for no and one for yes. Then try it with gestures for "No" or "Yes," but no actual words.

Students love this version, and it can lead to wonderful conversations about language, how to determine meaning, and what it would be like to move to a place where the people speak another language. It also is a good introduction to talking about nonverbal cues that occur—for example, when you visit a friend's house and you do something that you can tell the parent doesn't approve of by the look on their face or other nonverbal cue.

Combine with the Compliment Game (p. 112).

NOTES

If the student in the first game (negative reinforcement variation) gets frustrated and freezes, switch to positive reinforcement to help him or her find the object.

Yoga Calm Tools | 7
Guided Relaxations

Every morning, I teach a lesson in a classroom to help the students get off to a good start. We always do some breathing, a little stretching, and a short lesson on social/emotional skills. In this time I can also check in with the students to see if they are carrying emotions that may interfere with their day. Since some of the students in the class have troubled home lives, they often come in with unresolved anger or other emotions.

One morning, Jarad, a fifth grader, was making noises, playing with things on and around his desk, and working hard to distract the other students. Nothing I tried was working. I asked him to wait in the hall and to speak with me at the end of the session— at which point I asked him why his behavior was so difficult that day. He told me that the night before his father had brought friends over and his mother and father got into a big argument. He said they were very loud. Even after they had stopped arguing, he couldn't sleep because he was worried about them. Now he could barely keep his eyes open.

"That happens sometimes," I told him. "Arguments can occur in families, and when they do, it can be unsettling. It sounds like you need to sleep," I told him. "Why don't you go to the nurse's room and rest? You might have a better day after you sleep." He fell asleep the minute his head hit the pillow in the nurse's room and slept for two hours. Waking with a much better attitude, he had a good day.

The Importance of Rest

When we rest, the body heals and the mind and body integrate experiences. Rest allows us to reflect on the day and notice the effects of our activities on our emotions, mind, and body. In rest, free of distractions and stimulation, we are able to dream, to imagine, to work on solutions to our daily lives.

Sleep deprivation, on the other hand, can negatively affect mental performance, muscle control, and mood. Furthermore, strong, mounting evidence indicates that lost or damaged sleep is associated with serious long-term health problems including heart disease, diabetes, viral infection, cancer, depression, and substance abuse.

Adequate sleep and rest are important not only for growing bodies but also for mental development and emotional health. Scientists believe that sleep helps to weave disparate, emotionally fragmented, or weakly coupled memories together into coherent structures that the brain can then use more effectively during wakefulness. The more complex the physical or mental experience, the more important sleep is for efficiently integrating and remembering the experience.

Yet sleep and rest are seriously endangered in the lives of modern children. The National Sleep Foundation suggests that increasing demands from school, sports, and other extracurricular

129

and social activities are cutting into children's rest and sleep time. Similarly, in *Healing Night*, Rubin R. Naiman notes that, in recent years, the amount of sleep adolescents get has been reduced by two or more hours a night, and that the quality of their sleep has been eroded by television, videos, and other outside stimuli. As school-age children become more interested in TV, computers, and the Internet—and consume increasing amounts of caffeine—many develop problems with falling asleep, nightmares, and sleep disruptions. In particular, watching TV close to bedtime has been associated with bedtime resistance, difficulty falling asleep, anxiety around sleep, and sleeping fewer hours.

Suffice it to say, children must be given more opportunities to relax, rest, and rejuvenate.

Yoga Philosophy and Relaxation

Yoga philosophy has an interesting analogy of the sensory system that corresponds with modern theory on sensory integration: namely, what we take in through our senses is food for the brain. If we receive more stimulation than we can "digest"—if we don't have enough time to rest, for example, or if the sensory "food" we take in is not good for us—we start to get sick. This is partly why many yogic practices encourage self-reflection and relaxation—activities that are particularly important for children.

Therefore, one important practice in yoga is the relaxation pose that comes at the end of a yoga session. As B.K.S. Iyengar, a well-respected yoga teacher who has played a large part in bringing yoga to the West, states, "The stresses of modern civilization are a strain on the nerves for which [deep relaxation] is the best antidote."

In final relaxation at the end of a Yoga Calm session, students lie on their backs and allow their breath to return to a relaxed natural pattern. As the breath slows, the mind relaxes, allowing the body even greater release. This is often when students begin to connect with their deeper feelings—and when they have time to sort things out. As mentioned earlier, the relaxation response also helps to turn on the immune system and facilitates the body's growth. Thus, the relaxation poses are often considered the most important part of yoga in that they allow the mind, body, and emotions to heal, grow, and integrate.

Emotional Integration

Often, the mind will create all kinds of distractions to avoid coming into contact with the feelings and sensations that can come up during relaxations. If an uncomfortable thought, a disturbing sensation, or a memory begins to emerge, we can habitually create distractions to avoid these sensations. We take flight. But if a trusted teacher is available to help students move through these sensations, healing can occur.

> As the class prepared for the final relaxation, I asked the students what images they would like to have in their closing story. Steven asked for a dragon. He went on, "I want a fierce dragon. No, I want two dragons who are really strong, and I want them fighting with each other."
>
> Now, I try to keep the imagery peaceful in relaxations, but I know too that sometimes children request imagery with deeper meanings. Steven had been removed from his home when he was 5 and placed in foster care. He had a great deal of emotion around his biological mother and the experiences in her home. I said to him, "Wow, those dragons sound really upset. I wonder what they're so angry about?"
>
> His eyes widened as he said, "I know what they're angry about. Their mom left them, and they really miss her."

"I see," I responded. "I wonder what we can do to help them with their anger."

"I know!" he said excitedly, "A mommy dragon can come and take them back to her and then they will stop fighting!"

So in our imagery that day, we had two angry, fighting dragons, and a mommy dragon came. The two younger dragons were very happy to see her. They flew around in the sky together doing flips and glides, and then they flew off to Dragonland together. Steven lay very still on his mat, his eyes open, looking up at me as I told the story.

When we take time to listen to the imagery of children and explore it with them, we begin to understand their symbolic language. We see that there are important and often healing messages in their images, and we can help guide them through their fears and sorrows. When the adults in their lives are moving fast, and children can only recall images they've learned from the media, the personal, individual symbolism is buried. A parent or other adult can easily miss the significance of a child's dreams or imaginings.

For example, one evening when we were visiting some out-of-town friends, we all decided to watch a movie. The parents chose an extremely violent and graphic dramatization of war. Their children, who were in elementary school, watched wide-eyed. When Lynea asked the mother whether it ever bothered them to watch such violence, the mother assured her that the kids appeared completely unaffected by it. Yet the next morning, the daughter said that she'd had a nightmare. Her mother seemed not to hear, busy as she was with fixing breakfast. Lynea asked the girl what her nightmare was about. She said that she had been chased by angry men with guns. Her mother continued cooking, unaware of the significance of what her daughter was saying. Talking about this incident later, we wondered how many other times the girl had reported that movies had affected her sleep and her mother had missed the information.

Developing a Healthy Imagination

Cruelty and thoughtlessness on the part of the adults within the camp of any people can cause a child's dream vision to blur, and the dream can become a nightmare. But worse than this, the child will eventually cease to dream at all.

—Hyemeyohsts Storm, *Song of Heyoehkah*

Increased external stimulation and lack of rest are profoundly affecting the imagination of children and adults in the modern world. With so much external stimulation, and decreasing time to allow the imagination to roam, the inner, creative world is being buried. In *Healing Night,* Naiman expresses it this way:

Entertainment, the new opiate of the masses, mitigates the subtle ache and numbness symptomatic of our dream loss. Our innate hunger for the imaginative and creative sustenance of dreaming is now quelled with the processed and prepackaged images of television, movies, and video games. Are we unwittingly engaging the services of professional dreamers to do our dreaming for us?

Industrial culture has reduced imagination to a real-world commodity that can be mass produced, purchased, and consumed. Imagination has been abducted from its natural home in our hearts and is being held captive in theme parks, virtual reality games, movies, and television shows. Even the great big imagination of a really small child cannot compete with men in giant mouse suits. The entertainment industry's spiritual sleight of hand has drawn our vital energies away from the heart, from ourselves, from our personal dreams. We spend significantly more time attending to television than we do to our inner vision.

Among those concurring with this view is author David Sousa. In *How the Special Needs Brain Learns,* he writes, "A recent survey showed that children 10-17 years of age spend an average of 13.4 hours a week watching television and using computers, but only 47 minutes a week of quality time talking with their parents." According to the American Academy of Pediatrics, television viewing is directly associated with decreased homework time, quality time with parents or siblings, and time in creative play.

When a 2-year-old child learns that princesses look like the models on television, her opportunity to imagine herself as a princess is reduced. She begins at an early age to look outside of herself to understand how she should look and behave. When a child begins his young life with thousands of images of violence as a solution to anger, it is no wonder that young people increasingly express anger in violent ways. The idea of violent force is planted long before the child has an understanding of his or her own anger and fear. Pediatric physicians have been concerned about the impact of television programming on children and have made strong recommendations to parents, of which the American Academy of Pediatrics' guidelines for healthy parenting, reproduced below, are representative.

Guidelines for Healthy Parenting
from the American Academy of Pediatrics

1. Limit children's total media time (including entertainment media).

2. Remove television sets from children's bedrooms.

3. Discourage television viewing for children younger than 2 years, and encourage more interactive activities that will promote proper brain development, such as talking, playing, singing, and reading together.

4. Monitor the shows children and adolescents are viewing. Most programs should be informational, educational, and nonviolent.

5. View television programs along with children, and discuss the content. Two recent surveys involving a total of nearly 1,500 parents found that less than half of parents reported always watching television with their children.

6. Use controversial programming as a stepping-off point to initiate discussions about family values, violence, sex and sexuality, and drugs.

7. Use the videocassette recorder [or DVD player] wisely to show or record high-quality, educational programming for children.

8. Support efforts to establish comprehensive media-education programs in schools.

9. Encourage alternative entertainment for children, including reading, athletics, hobbies, and creative play.

Developing a healthy imagination is vitally important in the lives of children for many reasons. The imagination is the place where inventions are born, problems are resolved, and solutions begin to surface from the fabric of our lives. The imagination can give us a dream for the future and allow us to experience empathy. It is difficult to develop empathy if you're unable to imagine being in another person's shoes. In our imagination, we can place ourselves into a situation and create a solution before we are confronted with the real-life problem. Whenever one looks ahead to a frightening experience—a job interview, speaking in front of a class, competing in a race—the imagination works on strategies to manage the experience long before the event. Indeed, this act of "practicing for the event" is an important part of success. When children act out, through their bodies, the practice of being a strong man or woman, they are developing skills for self-protection and boundaries. In the lives of very young children, the imagination is their main tool for learning. They act out cooking, working, being a mom or dad. They use play and the imagination to express emotion and their symbolic language.

In addition, the imagination is a source of hope and beauty for surviving a difficult experience. Children of drug-addicted parents often create an imaginary picture of their parents to help them endure the hardships of their lives. They also imagine a different future to give them hope and the strength to keep living. The fantasy life of children in a very difficult environment can help carry them through the years when they have no power to change their circumstances. Later, when they are older and more capable of creating a life for themselves, the fantasy is no longer necessary and they can begin the hard task of facing the truth about their parents or their circumstances.

In Yoga Calm, we help children develop their imagination through specific exercises and guided relaxations. We also ask the students to look around the room and to notice the building, the desks, the computers—everything that humans have made. Then we remind them that every object first existed in someone's imagination before it was created. We stress that to achieve their dreams, they need to imagine their own future. We are careful to listen to their dreams and goals and to value their imagination. By allowing children both the time to explore their visions and the opportunity to express those visions to one another, we plant positive seeds for the future.

Leading Relaxations

Because modern children tend to be accustomed to being entertained, silent relaxations—like those at the end of an adult yoga class—do not work well for them initially. We've found that simple guided relaxations that include some sort of story help them relax more and develop their imagination.

Four guided relaxation techniques are especially effective, and they are suitable for both children and teens: Progressive Relaxations, One-Minute Explorations, Scripted Relaxations, and Personalized Relaxations in which the children's chosen images are woven into a story the teacher tells.

For all the relaxations, have the students sit at their desks or lie on their mats. At first, students may be more comfortable lying on their stomachs than on their backs, and some students can settle better if they are given a blanket. Ask the children to close their eyes and slow their breathing. Time them as they keep their bodies completely still for 30 seconds to a minute. These calming processes will help them prepare for guided relaxation.

Progressive Relaxations

Progressive Relaxations allow students to experience the contrast between tense and relaxed states by alternately tensing and relaxing specific muscle groups. By first tensing muscles, students become more aware of specific parts of the body, and the release afterward is deeper than if they were to simply try to relax. Here is a simple script for Progressive Relaxation that can be used with children:

Bring your attention to your feet. Now tense all the muscles in your feet. Hold the muscles tight for the count of four—1…2…3…4—then relax all the muscles in your feet.

Now bring your attention to your legs and tense all the muscles in your legs. Feel your legs lift off the floor and all your muscles activate. Hold them to the count of four—1…2…3…4—then relax. Feel your legs become soft, like Jell-O.

Now bring your attention to your belly. Make the muscles in your belly firm and strong and hold to the count of four—1…2…3…4—then release and relax.

Bring your attention to your back. Can you tighten the muscles in your back? What do you do to make your back muscles tight? Now hold the muscles strong to the count of four—1…2…3…4—then release and feel your muscles melt down your back.

Now bend your arms at the elbow and make the muscles in your arms hard like a weightlifter. Hold your arm muscles strong to the count of four—1…2…3…4—then release and take a deep breath.

Now make your hands into two fists. Clench them as tight as you can. Hold to the count of four—1…2…3…4—then release.

Now pull your shoulders up to your ears and feel your shoulder muscles tighten. Notice how it feels to tighten your shoulders. Now hold to the count of four—1…2…3…4—then completely release your shoulders and let your muscles melt like ice cream on a hot sidewalk.

Now bring your attention to your face and tighten all your facial muscles, scrunching up your eyes and your face like you have eaten something sour. Don't worry, no one is looking. Hold the muscles of your face to the count of four—1…2…3…4—then completely release. Relax your eyes, your mouth, your tongue.

Now with your whole body relaxed, take three long, slow breaths.

133

One-Minute Explorations

These short explorations—which can actually run as long as five minutes, as students' concentration and relaxation skills improve—not only enable students to be silent and relaxed, but also give them a focus for their quiet time. In classrooms, it can be nice to start the day with the positive thoughts that this activity encourages.

We usually begin with a one-minute vacation. Before starting, though, we turn off the lights and turn on quiet, soothing music. The students rest their heads on their desks or lie on their mats and can take themselves on vacation anywhere they want for one minute. Initially, you can help spark their imagination by offering several ideas about where they might go, what they could do, and so on. As the children get better at stillness, you can increase the time.

Below, you'll find more ideas for subjects to use for their imagination explorations.

Some Subjects for Imagination Exploration

- Remember a favorite time with a friend or family member.
- Imagine an invention that you can create.
- Go to your favorite vacation spot.
- Plan a party for yourself and your friends. What would you do? Where would you go?
- Think of three things you have done very well.
- Imagine creating a ride or game in an amusement park. What would it be like?
- Remember a sunny day when you were able to play outdoors with a friend.
- Think of three compliments you can give your class.
- Imagine the kind of day you would like to have today.
- Do you have a special place in nature or at your home? Imagine yourself there and picture what you like to do there.

Such explorations help students focus their minds on positive thoughts and can elicit positive emotions. They can also be used prior to specific lessons or writing assignments. For instance, before a history lesson, you could ask students to imagine traveling backward in time. Before a writing assignment in which they are to profile a friend, students might be asked to think of the person and the things he or she does. Before an art lesson, students could be asked to picture a flower or object in their mind's eye—or before an astronomy lesson, to travel to outer space and explore the planets.

By using the imagination, students prepare to learn prior to a lesson, and the class is calmer and more manageable. When children practice this kind of exploration regularly, they enjoy it and look forward to the few minutes of silence.

Scripted Relaxations

Scripted relaxations are guided relaxations that can be read to the class. One excellent resource for such relaxations is the book *Ready…Set…R.E.L.A.X.* We also include a sample script of our own at the end of this chapter.

When using scripted imagery, we recommend reading over the story before using it with children. Sometimes the scripts may have something questionable in them, or they may lead the students in a direction you had not intended.

When reading the script, it is important to go slowly enough to give students time to process the images and concepts presented. This "body time" is a little slower than the pace of reading a story aloud. Pause after the imagery and tune in to students' timing by watching their breathing, their bodies, and their facial expressions.

Another source for scripted relaxations is short picture books or children's poetry. One of our favorite books is *On the Day You Were Born,* by Debra Frasier. Other sources for scripted relaxations are short books or poems that provide plenty of visual imagery.

Personalized Relaxations

Personalized relaxations are short stories that you can create either ahead of time or on the spot. Children love stories that include people and things from their own lives, so we ask students to specify a person, place, or thing they would like in the story; then we weave these images into a journey. You may find it useful to write down their requests so you don't forget any, because the children will pay special attention to the story, anticipating the appearance of their images. Often, they request imagery that is important to their healing process. We have had students ask to include a father who is fighting in Iraq, a grandfather who has died, or a mother whom they haven't seen in a while. Creating these stories takes practice and creativity, but the outcome is well worth the effort.

The best way to begin is to start the journey where the students are now, then to come full circle, returning to the room at the end. In telling the tale, involve as many senses as possible—sensory details bring the children more completely into the experience. If the group is wound up, make it a slow, calming journey. If energy is low, use humor and play to bring the group back to a more wakeful, alert state. Either way, do keep the journey moving fairly quickly, to fit with children's sense of timing.

As you work your way through the narrative, you can engage your students' imagination by including additional choices in the imagery, referring to things like "your favorite food" or "your favorite animal." You can suggest they imagine bringing a friend along on the journey. Or you can use imagery and actions that provide a sense of control, such as the student taking a steering wheel or pressing buttons to guide a vehicle.

Use the journey as an opportunity to teach. Images such as warrior figures or animals can give the students messages about how to use their strength and skills in a positive way. Be careful not to turn those messages into a lecture, though! Just a few wise words from the child's character can be very powerful. In a similar vein, you could have the students find a gift or a treasure on their journey.

Sample Images to Weave into Your Guided Journeys

- Students riding on a magic carpet, as a starting point for the journey
- A teacher from the school doing something wild or funny
- A boat with soft pillows slowly floating down a green river
- Riding a dolphin into the ocean
- Finding a home where one of the children's characters lives
- Going to a karate training session where kids get to learn fighting techniques, then hear from the master how they are to use these new skills for good
- Student-provided images of a character performing a dance or magic tricks
- Arriving at a castle where the students are the kings and queens, and all their friends and relatives have come to a big party in their honor
- A garden where all the flowers are giant size

Personalized Relaxations can also be tailored to fit to specific curriculum needs or tied to academic activities. For instance, if you will be teaching a history lesson, you could take students back in time to see the place, people, events, and things they will later be learning about. If you will be teaching a science lesson, you could integrate facts about the subject area into the journey. We have found that this really stimulates interest and imagination!

Whatever imagery you use, remember to draw on your own imagination and life experiences and expertise. If you know about birds, include this knowledge. If you love music or dance, have people and things dance and play music. When you incorporate what you are passionate about, the journeys will have greater impact, and you will share more of yourself with your students.

Sample Relaxation Script: The Boat Ride

(Allow ten minutes for this journey)

Sit or lie comfortably with your eyes closed. Place your hands on your belly and feel your breath move up and down like waves in the ocean, rising and falling. Make the waves move up and down as slowly as possible.

In your mind, imagine that you are in a small boat. The boat is full of beautiful soft pillows. You can see the colors of the pillows, and you can feel their softness underneath you.

Feel the boat slowly rise up into the air. Now you are floating around the room in this wonderful little boat. You notice that in the boat there are three buttons. There's a green button, a yellow button, and a red button. When you push the green button, the boat moves a little faster. When you push the yellow button, the boat slows down. And when you push the red button, the boat stops and hovers in the air. You also notice that the boat has a steering wheel that is wooden and sturdy and just the right size for your hands.

You steer the boat out of the building and into the world outside. You float up above the trees and houses and people. You explore in your boat, turning left and right, pushing the green button to speed up and the yellow button to slow down. You might even try doing a few fancy moves up in the sky in your own private flying boat. You can feel the wind in your face and the warm sun shining on your back.

You begin to steer the boat over the trees and houses in the direction of the ocean. You come to the place where the ocean and land meet. You can smell the salty air and hear the seagulls squawking. Then you float out over the ocean. You can see the vast ocean beneath you, but you feel safe in your strong boat. Then, down below, you see a small island with a beach and a forest. You decide that you want to visit the island, so you gently steer your boat down and land it in the ocean near the island. Now you can feel the gentle rocking of the waves beneath you. The waves rock with the rhythm of your breath.

You steer the boat up onto the shore of the island. You take off your socks and shoes and step onto the beach. You can feel the coolness of the sand as it squishes between your toes. You walk along the shore of the beach, and you can hear the waves rolling into the shore.

You look into the trees and see a trail that leads into the forest. You walk up to the trail and follow it deeper into the trees. You can feel the soft earth under your feet, and you can smell the scented forest air. You walk along the path and come to a small cottage. There's soft music coming from inside the cottage, and your body tells you that this is a safe place. The cottage has a bright red door. You knock on the door, and when the door opens, you're surprised to find a person who is very important to you is inside. It may be a friend, a relative, or someone you have heard about in stories. The person smiles, invites you in, and serves you warm cookies and a fresh, cool drink.

The person says that they have invited you here because they have something important to tell you. So you sit and listen carefully to what the person has to say. (Pause for 15 to 30 seconds.) It feels good to be here with this person, and you thank them for their words.

Then you realize that it is time to go. You thank your friend for the cookies and the hospitality. You wave good-bye and travel back down the trail. There is your boat waiting for you. You push your boat into the water and climb in. You push the green button, and the boat lifts up into the air. You look down and you can see the cottage and the beach, and you know that you can return to this place any time you need to.

You float over the ocean and again see the place below where the land and the ocean meet. You fly over the trees and houses and cars until you come back to your building. You look down and you can see the rooftop and the door. You float down into the building and back into the room. As you settle down into your spot, the boat vanishes beneath you, and there you are again with your belly moving up and down with your breath.

Yoga Calm Tools
Emotional Guidance | 8

Let them take you.
Let them wrap their small fingers around yours.
Then follow them to the bug in the grass.
To the grave of their grandmother,
their sister,
their mother.
Meet their eyes when they look at you
with an expression full of difficult questions.
And when tears well up
in their big, beautiful young eyes,
breathe.
And listen.
They will tell stories
of dancing grandmas,
and sisters in heaven,
and mama bugs in the grass searching for their babies.
They will weave together a story of healing
as they pick small white daisies
and bright yellow buttercups
to decorate the grave
of the sister who died too soon.
And all they ask
is that you stay.
Stay strong.
As they laugh, and cry,
and celebrate their lives
through their stories,
their dances,
their small hands wrapped around yours.
God said, "A little child will lead them."
Now I understand.

—Lynea Gillen

> *" When emotional development lags behind cognitive development, the outcome can be a person who may be academically capable but unable to manage feelings of anger or fear. "*

The Need for Emotional Guidance

Using the Yoga Calm tools described earlier in this book can go a long way toward helping students learn about their emotions—how to express them, how to deal with them thoughtfully and responsibly. In particular, the social/emotional activities presented in chapter 6 provide numerous opportunities for students to develop the knowledge and skills needed for a successful life. But these are still practice opportunities, simulations. What happens when unexpected emotions bubble up or burst forth in the classroom, say? Or during a counseling session? The child then needs Emotional Guidance, or "emotional first aid"—support from a caring adult who understands how to acknowledge and appropriately respond to emotions in the moment.

Just as providing physical first aid means having some basic knowledge of the subject and training in how to help, so, too, with emotional first aid. It requires a basic understanding of the psychology of emotions, as well as training in how to respond to common situations.

In our hurried lives, we often give oversimplified solutions to emotional experiences. For instance, it's easy to instruct, "When you're angry, take a deep breath and count to 10"—but in fact, anger is far more complex than this. What happens after the ten seconds? There is a great deal to consider: What made you angry in the first place? Was it a person or an inanimate object? If it was a person, do you need to talk to him or her? If so, how do you talk about it without blaming and inciting more anger? And if you don't talk about it, will the situation continue? And what happens if you calm yourself down but the anger goes inside and simmers? Is the anger from the current experience or has the incident triggered some memory? The list of questions could go on and on—to the point where we are thoroughly overwhelmed! Fortunately, the tools of Emotional Guidance will help you discern what a teacher can do in the moment and when to refer to an expert.

Referring children for emotional or psychological help can be difficult, however, if your school lacks resources or parents are resistant. But referral is vitally important—just as with any other serious health or academic issue. For example, when a student is not progressing adequately in math or reading, the child's teachers and parents may suggest extra classes, outside tutoring, increased study time, or other actions to bolster the student's knowledge and skills. Yet if this same student is emotionally disconnected, feeling sad, or struggling with friendships, there are often few resources available. When counseling and adjunct resources are available, parents may be reluctant to send their children due to the stigma they feel exists about seeking emotional support. It's not at all uncommon to hear parents say things like, "My child really doesn't feel comfortable going to a counselor." As a result, children who aren't developing emotionally are often left to fend for themselves—at least until they get into severe enough trouble to be referred to the school counselor or an outside agency.

When emotional development lags behind cognitive development, the outcome can be a person who may be academically capable but unable to manage feelings of anger or fear. A very smart but angry student without an understanding of appropriate releases for his or her anger can become a very dangerous person in society. A quick glance at a newspaper shows any number of examples of smart adults who have not learned to manage their feelings and their impulses. One individual's greed leads him to a life of betrayal and embezzlement. Another's anger leads to a violent episode that destroys her family. Yet another person, unable to control sexual impulses, is caught soliciting teens on the Internet.

Educators who take a proactive approach—providing emotional first aid to all students as needed for everyday problems, and being a strong advocate for outside help for those with severe or chronic problems—can make a real difference. For in doing so, they help defuse situations early, improve classroom productivity, model for students, and provide early identification of children who are in trouble.

In this chapter you will find the perspective, key concepts, examples, and practical tools to enable you give your students the Emotional Guidance they need.

The Emotional Edge

While emotional triggers can spring from many sources, in yoga practice it is important to be aware that physical movement can generate emotional responses. The real power of yoga is not just about what we call the physical edge of the pose—the place where a person can hold the pose without injury and begin to open into new flexibility and strength. It is the recognition that the body has an emotional edge, too—the place where we become aware of and begin to heal past emotional trauma.

Past emotional traumas are stored in the body and can surface when we move in a new way. For instance, people who are physically capable of moving their shoulders may still hold grief in their heart that prevents them from opening completely to a particular posture. This is not to say that everyone who is inflexible has emotional trauma. Some people are just naturally less flexible than others. But it's important to keep in mind that yoga poses may trigger emotion that the individual wants to avoid. Thus, learning about the students and allowing them to express—and integrate—what they are feeling is an important tool in developing emotional awareness.

During our first round of practicing Volcano Breath (p. 97), Stuart moved expressively, just like the other students, bringing his hands to his heart, then opening his arms wide. Next I asked the students to close their eyes and imagine someone they would like to send their heart thoughts to, and we did Volcano Breath again. This time, Stuart's movements were dramatically different. I saw real pain in his face as he brought his hands to his heart. As he exhaled, his arms expanded in small, explosive, painful-looking movements. His eyes and mouth were squeezed shut.

When I asked after the activity if anyone would like to share, Stuart's hand shot up. I called on him first. In tears, he told the group that he had been thinking of his grandpa, who was very sick. When the other students asked, Stuart said his grandpa had been diagnosed with cancer. The students suggested repeating Volcano Breath so that they could send Stuart's grandpa thoughts of health. I told them to ask Stuart if that would be okay. He nodded.

The group practiced Volcano Breath again, this time sending their heart thoughts to Stuart's grandfather. Stuart's movements opened a little more and his face grew more peaceful. The group had supported him in his emotional need.

The ability to contain and direct the flow of thoughts and feelings into the conscious realm is a necessary life skill. No one wants to break down in grief in the middle of a lecture or at a party. Everyone needs to learn to manage the flow of emotion when it bubbles up, and the body is a large part of the management system.

Yet, in Yoga Calm, we also need to understand that it is possible to gain flexibility and strength in the poses and stay emotionally shut down by physically disconnecting—or dissociating—from the body. Some extreme athletes do this, pushing their bodies physically, ignoring the cues their bodies send. The danger is in developing the physical body without bringing the emotional body along. Over time, the person who practices yoga while dissociated not only risks physical injury but can begin to shut down to other important cues from the body. When people disconnect from their bodies, they are often shutting down to all feelings, including those of pain, thirst, hunger, and fatigue.

This kind of dissociation is necessary in war. Although the body is screaming to get out of the danger, the soldier has to dissociate from these messages in order to continue fighting. Children and adults who live in violent homes or neighborhoods learn to practice this form of dissociation as a survival skill. Indeed, everyone practices it to some degree to get through the trials of life. For instance, a widow who is raising three children does not have time to grieve the loss of her husband and may dissociate from her grief until she has time and space for it later in life. In many instances we have to put aside feelings to attend to the work at hand. If, however, a person continues to live in a dissociated state, never taking the time to listen to the body and feel the emotions that allow for release and healing, emotional and physical health are compromised. (For more about dissociation, see pp. 143 and 148.)

Emotional Guidance: Underlying Concepts

When children or adults break down emotionally, it can be frightening. This fear can be reduced by having a map to guide through the emotional storms, and the following discussion of concepts provides just such a map.

For, as a sign on one school counselor's door reads, "The only way out is through."

The Authentic Self, Ego, and Persona

The illustration below shows the relationships of some basic psychological concepts that we use in Yoga Calm. The outermost line represents the physical body, while the inner line represents the **ego boundary**. The ego boundary exists in both the mind and the body, and it operates as a protector. Its purpose is to maintain the balance of the individual personality by monitoring the information received from both the outer world and the inner world. As suggested previously, unconscious material can be released by moving the body.

physical body

ego boundary
the great protector

true self

Within the ego boundary is the **true self**: the part of us we turn to for guidance and understanding. It represents the full potential of the individual. In yoga philosophy, the true self is said to be as small as a grain of rice but more powerful than anything in the world.

Individual identity is seated in the **ego.** Ego expresses what is conscious, what the "I" knows. It is the gatekeeper between the conscious and the unconscious, which consists of all the images and other elements that are not yet known or understood by the ego. As mentioned, it's also the part of ourselves that protects and manages information from the outside and the inside world. For instance, if a sad memory begins to reveal itself in the middle of a job interview, the ego protects the individual by containing the memory so that the interview can continue without distraction. The ego also protects from the outer world. If, during an interview, something strange is happening outside the window, the ego acts as a shield to focus the individual away from the distraction. Many children with autism and ADHD do not have strongly developed egos, and their nervous systems are disrupted, so they may have an especially difficult time managing these inner and outer distractions.

When a traumatic memory is held in the body, the ego acts as a boundary to keep the memory from breaking into the conscious mind, and this can sometimes develop into a rigid physical posture in a certain area of the body. An overdeveloped ego can create a rigid personality.

The **persona** is one's public personality, the image that one puts out into the world to mediate between inner and outer experiences. If an individual listens to dreams and imagery from the unconscious, the persona is more aligned with the internal sense of self. When the persona is in line with the authentic self, the person comes across to others as genuine. If, however, an individual ignores or denies his or her inner thoughts and feelings, the persona projects a feeling of deception and falseness.

Reenactment, Dissociation, and Flooding

In addition to these ways of talking about aspects of an individual's psychology, three processes are also useful to understand: reenactment, dissociation, and flooding.

Reenactment is a process in which people place themselves into situations that repeat a certain pattern in their lives. Often the reenactment drive originates in the unconscious. As the person brings awareness to the unconscious drive and expresses and understands the emotions that arise, the pattern begins to shift.

In our view, reenactment is an opportunity to heal. When an individual experiences something traumatic as a child, it is often held with a child's perception of the incident. By entering a similar experience as an adult, the individual can understand things from an adult perspective and heal from the earlier trauma. Often children reenact patterns through friendships; if they learn to understand this, they can begin to heal before they engage in a lifelong pattern of poor relationships.

This is important information for educators because, often, children do not choose to act out a negative pattern; they are trying to heal from an experience. For instance, Lynea once worked with a sixth-grade boy whose mother had left him when he was small—and who had become obsessed with "going out" with girls who were cruel to him. He would bend over backward for these girls, and they would always "dump" him. He was a smart boy, though, and as Lynea talked to him about the wound he had from the loss of his mother, he began to understand why he was acting out, and he learned new behaviors that eventually would help him succeed in relationships.

As mentioned, some people may avoid feelings by dissociating. **Dissociation** is a psychological defense mechanism in which specific, anxiety-provoking thoughts, emotions, or physical sensations are separated from the rest of the psyche. The dissociation can also involve separating from the body to prevent memories from resurfacing.

Flooding stands at the opposite extreme. In this process, an unconscious memory or feeling breaks through the ego boundary and fills the individual with emotion that is difficult to endure. The emotion is out of proportion to the event currently taking place.

Reenactment, Dissociation, Flooding—What They Look Like

A teacher asked me to go to the cafeteria, where I found a sixth-grade boy curled up in a fetal position in a corner of the kitchen and refusing to move. Knowing this student and something about his traumatic background, I told him I thought he was experiencing a flashback. I assured him that I would help him and invited him to my room so he wouldn't have to cry in the kitchen. He came with me willingly.

Closing the doors and the shades in my room and covering him with a blanket, I reassured him that he was in a safe place and I would stay with him. I told him that I thought he was experiencing a memory and that if he shared images as they came into his head, we could talk about them. His crying began to slow and his breathing returned to normal.

Eventually he took the blanket off and looked up, appearing exhausted. He said he thought he knew what happened. When he lived with his stepfather, an angry man, he would often get in trouble. To punish him, his stepfather would hold his hand under hot water. Today, as he was washing dishes in the school kitchen, the hot water hit his hand and memories of his stepfather came flooding into his conscious mind faster than he could handle them.

He and I worked together for several months on the memories of his stepfather. Years later, he returned for a visit before going off to study psychology in college. I'm sure he will be a fine and compassionate psychologist.

Integrating Store and Mind Consciousness

Understanding both the unconscious and the conscious is an important aspect of integrating emotional experiences in the Yoga Calm process. In Eastern philosophy, the unconscious is described as the store consciousness, and the conscious is the mind consciousness—two parts of the mind that cannot be separated. You can visualize the relationship between them by thinking of a house. In the illustration on page 144, the house represents the mind consciousness. Here we keep things like our daily schedule, the names of our friends . . . all the information essential to our daily lives. Below the visible house is the basement. This represents the store consciousness, full of memories and stories that are part of our lives—information that we can go down and retrieve, or that can come rushing up unannounced when triggered.

Importantly, the store consciousness holds information not only from an individual's personal life but also from past generations and one's culture. A person's store consciousness may hold stories of a grandfather who served in World War II, for example. There are also media images, trademarks, songs, and stories from one's culture and history. We see an image of the Nike swoosh and know what it symbolizes. We hear "The Star-Spangled Banner" and know its national and cultural significance. This is the stuff of collective knowledge.

community · routine · structure · safety

mind consciousness

negative seeds

positive seeds

store consciousness

The store consciousness also holds many seeds. The seeds are thoughts, attitudes, stories, and behaviors that we have been told or have seen modeled. These seeds, planted by parents, teachers, and other members of the community, can be either positive or negative. For instance, a child may have a relative who was a famous artist; the child looks to that person with a sense of pride and inspiration. There may just as well be a relative who was an alcoholic who wreaked havoc on the family; that person may be a source of fear or embarrassment, with parents and children alike worrying that this seed of alcoholism may grow in the family.

One of our goals in Yoga Calm is to plant and strengthen positive seeds and provide support and education about the negative seeds that have already been planted. If, for instance, alcoholism is present, it is not effective to push that memory away in the basement of the house. To do this can actually strengthen the seed's power. Secrecy develops fear and curiosity, and may in fact draw a person toward that seed. Consider the phrase, "Don't think of a brown bear." Immediately, the mind goes to the image, however hard you try not to think about it.

At the same time, it is important not to overemphasize a seed by discussing it daily—which can also add power to a negative influence. Telling the story of alcoholism over and over in a family system strengthens the fear and belief that the pattern will be repeated.

The idea in Yoga Calm is to acknowledge the negative seeds, allow the feelings to emerge, then plant many positive seeds to help the individual walk a path leading toward a constructive rather than destructive lifestyle.

A fifth-grade girl came into my office from the playground after losing control of her anger and exploding at another student. She sat down and cried, feeling defeated and ashamed. Saying "No one is as bad as I am," she referred to herself as a "delinquent," uttering the word as if it were some strange disease.

"Why do you say that?" I asked.

"Because my mother says that to me all the time and tells me that I am just like my father. He's in jail, and he was a delinquent. She says I'll probably turn out just like him."

"What do you think a delinquent is?" I asked.

"I don't know," she responded, "but I think it's a bad person who goes to jail. That's what my dad is, and that's what my mom says I'm going to be." Her father was in prison for violence, and she said he had a bad temper. I acknowledged that she had a temper too, but I pointed out that she was also passionate and very spirited. When someone was being mistreated, she was the first to jump in and protect others.

"It sounds like your father didn't get the support he needed to learn to manage his temper," I told her. "Maybe he wasn't taught to express his anger in appropriate ways." She explained that her grandfather used to hit her father with a belt and that her father had been kicked out of his home when he was a teenager. I began to see the seeds in the ancestry of this girl. Together, we drew a family tree and identified others in her history. There were many people she cared for and who supported her. Her father had a big red circle around him, representing the one person in her life whom she feared.

Over the years, we continued to work on her fiery nature. We created stories to help her learn how the fiery part could be put to good use. We read stories of Dr. Martin Luther King Jr., who expressed deep anger but was able to channel it toward change in the world. We talked about Mothers Against Drunk Driving, an organization that uses the very word M.A.D.D. to define itself. Its members learned to acknowledge their anger, then use it toward a positive goal. In yoga, she practiced listening to her Strong Voice (p. 122) and began to learn to manage this strong emotion inside of her. We planted many positive seeds for the future to help her ward off the image of herself becoming a "delinquent" like her father.

Many children have been told about the "bad" things that relatives have done without ever being given the rest of the story. But when a negative seed is allowed to emerge as in the story above, it can help a student understand why they are thinking and behaving in a way that is not good for them. How did this develop? What created it? Are there things one can do to prevent it? What kind of environment will help prevent this from happening again? These are the kinds of questions that need to be explored with children. The practice of developing strong, healthy hearts, minds, and bodies needs to be a daily opportunity. The more often we plant seeds of health and well-being, the greater the chance that these will grow.

By the same token, when yoga and positive thinking are practiced without allowing the negative feelings to emerge, or practiced with a desire to achieve perfection, there is a danger that the practice will become rigid and self-righteous. When people cannot be present with aspects of themselves that they consider undesirable, they may find it difficult to tolerate these qualities in others. They may look down on others and develop an air of superiority. But if we practice yoga with an understanding of human qualities and shortcomings, compassion and understanding grow. Great teachers in all traditions have been great because they were able to identify with and have compassion for all of humanity. Perhaps it was this very quality that allowed them to share their knowledge, wisdom, and selves so powerfully and effectively. If so, then we ourselves may become excellent teachers as we, too, learn how to express our compassion.

Using Archetypes in the Yoga Calm Process

The children scrambled to find a personal space in the room and squatted down ready to play the Archetype Game (p. 105). The fluorescent lights were off, and the room was lit only by a lamp and some daylight coming through the windows. The children had never played this game before, and they eagerly waited for instructions.

I told them, "I'm going to count to five, and you're going to grow into an angry statue. Then, when I turn on the music, we are going to let our angry selves out to share with one another.

"There are a few rules. It's not okay to touch anyone else, and you can't scream or run. You can growl or howl softly, though, like a dog or cat when they're giving a warning. Are you ready?"

"No!" Barton exclaimed, looking suddenly frightened. "You don't want to see my anger, Mrs. Gillen. I might hurt someone! I don't think this is a good idea!"

"I won't let you hurt anyone, Barton," I assured him. I knew this child well enough to trust that he could handle this game. "I will stay close to you. And if you start to feel out of control, we'll stop, okay?" He gave me a wide-eyed nod.

We grew into angry statues and looked around the room at the different faces of anger. Barton cautiously showed his teeth. Then I instructed the children to move around the room, expressing their angry selves. We leaped and growled and crawled into corners. We froze and began to sneak up on one another.

At first, Barton was very cautious, but soon he joined the game with his whole body. He and I hissed at each other and swiped at each other with imaginary swords. We laughed and growled quietly. Then we froze and slowly crept back to a circle to discuss the experience. But before we got there, Barton shouted out, "Can we do that again? That was great!"

I smiled and said, "Yep, you let your angry self out, and you didn't hurt a soul."

During the sharing time, Barton described how his anger had often gotten him into trouble and reported that his mother and father told him many times that he needed to keep his anger in. We talked about how anger isn't a bad thing. It's just important to learn to use it in the right way.

The use of archetypes can be especially beneficial in Yoga Calm practice, helping children to explore and integrate the various aspects of themselves in a safe and healthy way.

Archetypes, as you may know, are motifs or images that universally appear in stories and art. They represent different aspects of the self. The image of the warrior, the divine child, the orphan, the wise one—these are all archetypes that represent different aspects of the human experience. Fairy tales and myths are powerful because they represent these and other fundamental but different parts of the personality and the struggles that occur when we encounter them in life. The stories teach us that the trickster can be both useful and dangerous, and that the path to becoming a warrior involves facing hardship. They are psychological teaching stories that guide and help integrate the varied parts of ourselves. We can relate to the young child who longs to prove her competence as a warrior, queen, or brilliant musician. We have empathy for the fool who is trying his best and failing at every turn. By stepping into the story, we gain compassion and understanding for ourselves and others.

Many of the students who come to counseling have been separated from parts of their personalities. Perhaps they have come from a powerless family situation and have had few opportunities to experience being warriors. Or their family life is so chaotic and disrupted that they have never enjoyed the experience of feeling like a safe and divine child. Many students have not had an adult in their life who could tolerate the playful trickster inside, nor their aggressive hero, so they feel ashamed of these parts of themselves. By using the archetypes in yoga, however, students can play with different parts of their personalities. As they practice using their strength, it becomes more available to them in their daily lives, and they gain skill and understanding about the importance of strength in the human experience—just as by practicing the qualities of other archetypes, children can learn how to use the different parts of their personalities constructively. By embodying archetypes and exploring them safely, children can get to know previously unacceptable aspects of themselves without coming to harm. As we saw with Barton, above, students having a newly positive experience long to recreate it. Such play can guide them toward a holistic understanding of the many roles we must play in order to have safe and successful lives.

Processing Emotions

Because children are just learning to edit their thoughts, they will sometimes blurt out intimate details of their lives. This can happen during a lesson on families, or when the teacher is reading a story, or on the playground—whenever and wherever a feeling emerges. Children who have experienced trauma can be triggered by many things, and since they spend a great deal of time in school, these feelings inevitably arise during the school day. For girls or boys who have been abused, a compliment from another student or a student accidentally brushing against them can act as a trigger. A mean word or angry look from a child at recess can trigger a memory of verbal abuse from a parent or loved one. A simple question can bring up intense feelings in a child.

> *First-grader Ryan was curled up in a ball on the playground, crying. He had told another boy that he "wanted to die and go to heaven to see his father." I found Ryan surrounded by students with looks of concern and fear on their faces. They all began telling me what had happened. I thanked them for their concern and told them I would help him. I asked Ryan to come into my room and talk to me.*

> *Knowing that at the age of two Ryan had watched his father die of a heart attack, I was aware that he was grieving his father's death. He said that the other boys were talking about their dads, and one of them asked him his father's name. He told the boys that his father was in heaven and he wouldn't see him again until he died. That's why he wanted to die and go to heaven.*

> *I listened to Ryan's feelings and allowed him to share what he knew about his father. We called his mom to tell her he was having a sad day, and she told him they would talk about it when he got home.*

> *Later that week, Ryan brought in pictures of his father, and we started a book about him so Ryan could hold his father in his heart. In Yoga Calm sessions, Ryan now sends his heart thoughts to his father when we practice Volcano Breath (p. 97). This way he can be close to his father in his daily life.*

How adults respond to incidents like Ryan's demonstrates how we regard emotion. If we ignore these experiences, the students may conclude that their emotions are not important and may begin to shut them down. But when we acknowledge and support their emotions, they feel safe and well cared for. Like Ryan, they learn that their emotions are valid and that there are adults in the world who will stay with them when they need emotional support.

Acknowledging Emotion, Providing Support

As we were practicing Volcano Breath (p. 97) and thinking of someone to whom we would like to send our heart thoughts, Trudy, a fourth-grader, began to cry. At first she cried lightly, but soon she was sobbing deeply. After I stopped the group and asked the students to sit in a circle, Trudy told us she was worried because her mom had begun using drugs again. I reminded the group of the confidentiality rule: what's said in group stays in group. I wanted Trudy to feel that what she had just shared would not be broadcast on the school playground.

We spent the rest of the class time talking about worries and ways we can care for ourselves when we are worried. Some students expressed concern about parents, school troubles, or friends. The students each identified someone in their life whom they could go to when they were worried. I told Trudy that we would talk privately after class if she needed more support. We closed with a guided relaxation that included the people in our lives who support us during times of worry.

Although we recognize that teachers and parents cannot be expected to be counselors, a basic understanding of emotional care is essential when working with children. Emotional care may be the most overlooked need in modern society. Though many self-help books and magazines promise to improve relationships and bring happiness, the daily practice of emotional care is often absent. When a single parent or two parents work full time, they may have little time to take care of the emotional needs of either themselves or their children. If a child expresses a deep feeling, you may hear parents exclaim, "There's no time for this!" And in our fast-paced culture, it's true that there is often very little time for emotional processing.

The structure of the school day doesn't lend much opportunity for emotional processing either. Because of the emphasis on accelerating academic learning, it is difficult to get students out of class for longer than a half hour for counseling group work, even if the work is supporting a child's total well-being. Lynea likes to tell of a time when she was working with a group and found herself rushing along a sixth-grade girl who had been expressing her feelings about her parents' recent divorce. Finally, Lynea said, "Okay, finish up! I don't want you all to be late for class." That's when another student chimed in to put things into perspective.

"We're trying to share our feelings here, Mrs. Gillen! You'd think they'd give us an hour a week to share our feelings!"

Feelings are not obedient aspects of the self that wait to emerge until after yoga class or the end of a school day when students are safely tucked away in the privacy of their home. They can emerge during class, in the middle of a science lesson, working on an art project, or while you're reading a story. Responding appropriately to emotion is a necessary skill—necessary for teachers, counselors, and other professionals who work with children, as well as for each of us in our daily lives.

There are many teachers who find time to listen to students and support their emotional needs, but often teachers report that the emotional needs are taking a great deal of time and students are unable to focus because they are worried about problems at home. Again, when teachers, parents, and family members are too busy to listen, they may unintentionally send messages to children that their emotional needs are unimportant. Children attempt to handle the emotion for each other on the playground, and they do the best they can, but it is a big job for a second grader to assist a student who is crying because they have lost a parent or because their parents are divorcing. Children need adult support when these emotions arise. They need the emotional first aid that Emotional Guidance can provide. We need to make the time for it.

While I was substitute teaching in a kindergarten classroom, another kindergarten teacher approached me during recess. Knowing I was working toward my counseling degree, she asked me about a student in her class. She pointed out a quiet boy who was playing by himself on the playground. He appeared lonely. The boy, whose father had died of cancer over the summer, had been withdrawn and quiet for the three months since the school year had started. The teacher wondered whether the loss of his father had something to do with it. She asked if I knew anything about young children and death.

I suggested that she gently bring up the subject of death with the children. I mentioned some wonderful children's books, such as The Dead Bird, *that deal with death in a simple, childlike way. She responded with deep concern. "Oh, I can't do that! Isn't there an expert who can come in and talk to the children about this? I don't want to bring it up with the student." But the school had no counselor, and I didn't know of anyone who could come into the school and talk to the children about death. Also, I thought it would be inappropriate for someone the children didn't know to come in and discuss such a delicate subject.*

I felt concern for the child who struggled alone with his loss. I thought about how this child was dealing with the reality of his father's death every day while his teacher was uncomfortable with the subject and the school had no counselor. I left hoping that this young boy would find someone who could listen to his sorrow.

What is crucial in developing yoga for children is to create a practice that understands children's developmental needs physically, mentally, and emotionally. When we actively teach concepts such as compassion, personal responsibility, self-care, community service, and communication skills, students can practice the integration that yoga sets out to teach. By allowing children to discuss their emotions in an appropriate and respectful way, we educate them about emotional needs. The practice becomes deeper and more meaningful for students, teachers, and counselors.

Responding to Dissociation and Emotional Triggers

When something triggers a student's emotions, those emotions may manifest physically. For instance, you may see that a student is showing extreme resistance to particular poses. You may notice rigidity or the student holding his or her breath. A list of typical physical signs of emotional distress appears below. While these signs may likewise alert you that a student is dissociating, dissociation doesn't always occur. Nor is dissociation always negative. It is a natural and necessary part of life.

Physical Expressions of Dissociation and Emotional Triggers

- Extreme resistance to particular poses (without a physical injury)
- Holding a specific part of the body in an overly stiff or unnatural way (in the absence of injury)
- A military or rigid approach to poses
- Holding the breath
- A glazed or distant look in the eyes
- An upward gaze
- Extreme agitation
- Inability to follow directions in a particular pose
- An unwillingness to participate in relaxation poses
- Extreme silliness or a flippant attitude about particular poses
- A feeling of superiority and an unwillingness to identify with the common person

What should you do if a student's emotions are triggered during a Yoga Calm session or if you believe a student is dissociating? For one thing, you can simply slow down the process a bit. You can give the student words or images to help get through the situation, such as positive self-talk (Ground Rules, p. 42). You can define the trigger to the student, saying something like, "That's the part of you that wants to give up. Let's see if we can help that part get stronger so that it'll want to keep going." You can switch to a less triggering pose. If the student is agitated, you can allow him or her to lie down in a relaxation pose. Counselors can use group process techniques to deal with the situation, while noncounselors can use the group to strengthen the student by giving positive feedback or having the other students talk about what they do to help them through sad, mad, or scared times. Yet another alternative is to simply ask the student to stay and talk to you after class. Sometimes, a combination of two or even three of these techniques may be most effective.

But what if a child fully breaks down in sorrow, anger, or pain? Witnessing this can be very difficult, and it is helpful to have a few tools at hand when this occurs in a classroom. Some basic communication skills are helpful, as shown in the Communication Game (p. 109). The communication skills of reflecting feelings, paraphrasing, and asking questions are helpful to everyone yet are especially important as counseling tools. Below are some additional tools for providing Emotional Guidance, or emotional first aid, during crisis.

Tips on Administering Emotional First Aid

- Listen. It's one of the most powerful healing tools that exist.

- Avoid the instinct to give advice or try to fix the problem.

- Remain calm. When a child is upset, he or she will cue off the body signals sent by the adult. If the adult is upset, it can translate to children that their emotions are a bother or are upsetting to the adult.

- Ask the child to use the Yoga Calm strategies they have learned, particularly Grounding, finding Stillness (see chapter 2), and working with the breath (see chapter 4 and the breathing exercises in chapter 5).

- Help the student find a place where he or she can be alone. Some teachers have created "cool down" spots in their classrooms where students can be alone and work with Play-Doh or draw while they bring their emotions under control.

- If the child needs someone to talk to and no one is available, schedule a time later in the day when he or she can talk to either you or the counselor. If this is not possible, help the student identify someone who can listen—a grandparent, parent, older sibling, or other relative. Sometimes a peer who has been through a similar experience can be helpful (e.g., another child who has experienced divorce and has stabilized).

- If a student shares memories or information that is beyond the scope of the classroom, refer him or her to the school counselor or psychologist. If the school has no counselor, provide referrals to the family and encourage the parents to get support for their child. It is helpful to keep a list of local resources on hand.

- Know your limits. Some teachers are skilled and comfortable talking to students about their emotions and their family life. If, however, you are uncomfortable with something the child brings up, be honest and find another adult who can support the child.

- Some emotion may look trivial to the adult, but in many cases, a memory has been unearthed, and the child's deep emotional reactions are sincere. Avoid saying things like "Get over it." It is more effective to ask, "What strategies can you use to help you through this?" or "What helps you feel better when you're upset?"

- Model that it's okay to have emotions, and educate the other students. Say things like "Johnny's feeling a little upset right now, so he's going to take care of himself." Allowing the class to process the experience is helpful if a classmate has been visibly upset.

Letting the class process the experience of a student's distress can provide powerful learning moments, as when Lynea once assisted in an Outdoor School experience.

> *As the students climbed into their bunks, one boy, feeling homesick, became extremely upset. He was crying hard and breathing with short, shallow gasps. This triggered fear in several of the other students. They asked what was wrong with the boy, if he was having an asthma attack, if he was going to die. Lynea calmly told the group that he was feeling very homesick and he was upset, but his teacher was coming and she would help him feel better. After the teacher came, the group spent a few minutes talking about times they felt homesick and things they did to help them get through it. This short discussion helped to calm the other children in the cabin.*

Cultivate Healthy Emotional Skills, Cultivate a Healthy Future

In the past, coal miners would test for oxygen in the mines by sending down canaries to test the air. In a way, children may be seen as the canaries of our culture. The numbers of students coming to school with anxiety, ADHD, depression, and a host of other health problems is a warning sign to us about the emotional health of our society.

Lorne Ladner notes as much in *The Lost Art of Compassion:*

> On a cultural level, when our negative emotions such as hatred, greed, jealousy and rage are not addressed and counterbalanced by strong positive values and emotions, this can result in many destructive events. . . . Too often, our prevention begins at the line of last defense. . . . To the extent that we feel caring and connected with each other in our homes, schools and corporations, we naturally refrain from harmful behaviors. Empathy and compassion are foundational for natural ethics and for positive social relationships.

Fortunately, tools such as compassion, empathy, and understanding can be taught at an early age, as can the ability to understand, process, and manage emotions. Health and wellness depend on it—our children's health and our own and that of our culture. After all, children are our future.

Truly, a deep beauty emerges when members of a community share their sorrows and joys. Research shows that addressing the emotional needs and developing the emotional skills of children enriches their lives, increases their academic ability, and builds resiliency. The public schools are ripe with opportunities to develop strong, compassionate children and communities. And, as Ladner also reminds us, "By understanding how our emotions work, we can stop cultivating negative emotions and begin habituating ourselves to positive emotions. The more time and energy we invest in cultivating positive emotions, the more spontaneous and powerful they will become, ensuring happiness for ourselves and those around us."

Class Planning
Putting It All Together | 9

Yes, there is a lot to Yoga Calm! And while the primary purpose of this book is to provide you with an in-depth understanding of this method, we also include activities and class plans that you can use tomorrow with your students. Ultimately, the vision for this book, and for our work, is to empower you—to help you creatively apply yoga, social/emotional learning, and your own talents and gifts in the service of children. With an understanding of the principles, purpose, and power of this work, now is the time to put it *to* work.

Getting Started

You need not have a significant amount of experience with yoga or be physically "in shape" to begin teaching Yoga Calm. Many activities—such as the breathing, social/emotional learning activities, and relaxation techniques—can be taught by anyone. In addition, the physical yoga and balancing poses are designed to be safe and accessible for people with a wide range of abilities. However, we do recommend a home yoga practice and classes with an experienced teacher to develop your comfort and knowledge in the physical and mental aspects of this wellness practice.

Regardless of your experience in practicing yoga, you will want to start slowly and simply with your students. Pick one or two Yoga Calm activities, practice them yourself, and then introduce them to your class. Teachers can use Upward Mountain and Crescent Moon (p. 96) for a great midday stretch break in the classroom, and counselors will find Belly Breathing (p. 63) with the Hoberman Sphere, followed by Pulse Count (p. 83) and Volcano Breath (p. 97), an effective way to prepare students for a counseling group. But whatever you start with, **use these same activities daily if possible, or at least several times a week, creating a routine and structure for students.** Later, you can add to the routine or vary it for interest.

We have included minimum recommended activities and their frequency in Appendix A, Yoga Calm Curriculum Recommendations for Classroom Teachers.

According to the American Council on Exercise, "Children should start out slowly with an exercise program that is interesting and fun to them. By beginning a program gradually, children can decrease the risk of injury and lowered self-esteem that could result from unrealistic goals." Ultimately, we should encourage students toward the activity levels recommended by the Centers for Disease Control and Prevention: 60 minutes or more of moderate-intensity physical activity each day, including some exercise occurring in several 10- to 15-minute bursts of moderate to vigorous activity.

Basic Class Plans

While Yoga Calm activities can be used individually—for example, using a single activity as an energizer before a test—they are most effective when combined into a sequence, or flow. The four sample sequences shown on the following pages are arranged by the time they take, from five to twenty minutes. Each meets our curriculum recommendations and fits a broad range of student ability and class situations. See chapters 5, 6, and 7 for specific instructions on each pose or activity depicted.

Looking at these Basic Class Plans, you may notice that each sample flow follows an **energy cycle from calm to active and back to calm**. We have validated this basic sequencing approach through many years of teaching yoga to various populations; it is spelled out in more depth on p. 160. In sum, this cycle allows students the opportunity to transition, calm themselves, and focus so that they can perform the physical activities with better control and with more physical, mental, and emotional awareness. It provides students with practice in how to regulate their nervous systems, whether it be energizing or calming. And it allows them the opportunity to develop their imagination, to rest, and to integrate their experience come at the beginning and end of each sequence.

Looked at another way, each of these flows applies all five Yoga Calm principles: Stillness, Listening, Grounding, Strength, and Community. While the first four are obviously manifested in the physical poses, principles of Community are more implicit. Yet we practice them in a variety of ways: by respecting each other's space (part of the Ground Rules; see p. 42); by having students take turns leading the sequences; by facilitating and guiding the sharing that can occur after Volcano Breath and relaxations; and by breathing, moving, and working together. Time permitting, additional social/emotional learning processes (see chapter 6) can be added to each Basic Class Plan. We recommend adding these after the more physically active poses and before the twists and final relaxation.

As a basic framework for introducing Yoga Calm, these flows provide comprehensive benefits for students and are relatively easy to teach. And by **focusing on a theme such as Strength or Stillness**, even a familiar sequence can reveal new depth. Later, you can add variations, more advanced poses, and other activities as you become more familiar with the method and as your students' abilities increase.

Remember: it is not the pose but how we work with it that is most important.

This quick, easy, and effective flow calms, focuses, energizes, and prepares students for learning—in just five minutes! Use it at the beginning of the day, for transitions, and as a "sponge" activity when you have extra time to fill. The One-Minute Exploration can be lengthened by adding a theme to engage the imagination for the class lesson topic or creative projects of any kind, further uniting Yoga Calm with your particular curriculum.

YOGA CALM QUICK 5

CALM

Seated Belly Breathing

Seated Pulse Count

ACTIVE

Warrior I

CALM

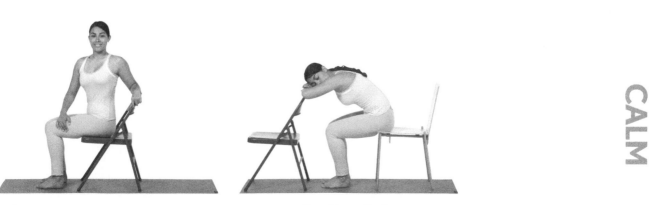

Twist

One-Minute Exploration

155

YOGA CALM TOP 10

Another excellent learning-preparedness process, this 10-minute flow emphasizes more standing and balancing poses, which have an energizing and grounding effect. It's a good flow for those afternoon lulls and to help develop the calm-yet-energized state necessary for test-taking. Volcano Breath can be especially helpful in determining and releasing emotions that may inhibit the learning process.

CALM

Seated Belly Breathing

Seated Pulse Count

Volcano Breath

ACTIVE

Woodchopper

Mountain

Roots

Crescent Moon

Modified Dancer

CALM

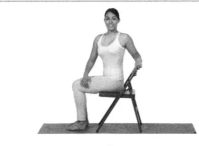

Twist

One-Minute Exploration

This 15-minute flow lets you start where you are by using your classroom's chairs and tables to support your students' exploration of yoga. Accessible to a wide range of abilities, the Chair 15 promotes flexibility, strength, and balance. The middle portion of the flow, from Mountain to second Mountain can be led by students and performed several times in a row to improve fitness. According to the Centers for Disease Control and Prevention and the American College of Sports Medicine, small bouts of activity, even 10 minutes at a time, count toward daily physical education standards.

YOGA CALM CHAIR 15

CALM

Seated Belly Breathing   Seated Pulse Count   Volcano Breath

ACTIVE

Mountain   Upward Mountain   Forward Bend   Lunge (right leg back)

Upper Lunge   Chair Dog   Lunge (right leg forward)   Upward Lunge

Forward Bend   Chair   Upward Mountain   Mountain

CALM

Twist   One-Minute Exploration

YOGA CALM MAT 20

This comprehensive 20-minute flow is designed for a PE class, counseling session, or classroom where there is room for yoga mats. It promotes fitness, flexibility, strength, and balance. The middle portion of the flow, from Mountain to second Mountain, can easily be led by students (with the teacher giving the verbal cues). Perform it several times in a row to provide additional physical exercise. Adding a Yoga Calm social/emotional learning activity or a game where Tree pose is in the sequence can also provide additional student motivation. According to the Centers for Disease Control and Prevention and the American College of Sports Medicine, small bouts of activity, even 10 minutes at a time, count toward daily physical education standards.

CALM

Belly Breathing

Pulse Count

Leg Stretch

Rock and Roll

Boat

Volcano Breath

ACTIVE

Mountain

Upward Mountain

Forward Bend

Bent Knee Lunge (right leg back)

Downward Dog

Plank

Cobra

Downward Dog

Bent Knee Lunge (right leg forward)

Forward Bend

Chair

Upward Mountain

Mountain

Tree

ACTIVE

Twist

Relaxation

CALM

Advanced Class Planning Formula:
Themes, Principles, and Social/Emotional Learning

Any effective Yoga Calm flow or Basic Class Plan follows a well-defined pattern:

CALM

1. Always start with a Stillness or calming activity to help students center and focus their attention. Belly Breathing (p. 63)—alone or aided by using a Hoberman Sphere—is great for this, and children like the consistency of starting the same way every time.

2. Continue by leading Pulse Count (p. 83), a balance pose, or grounding activity that promotes Listening and/or Grounding—introspection, focus, and physical awareness.

ACTIVE

3. Combine two or three poses into a sequence, or use a pose flow that warms, energizes, and develops Strength, flexibility, and fitness.

4. Continue with a Community-building activity or social/emotional activity.

CALM

5. End with another Listening or Stillness activity such as Child (p. 70) or Twist (p. 95), followed by an integrating experience such as a One-Minute Exploration (p. 134) or Personalized Relaxation (p. 135).

With this formula and a basic knowledge of Yoga Calm activities, and the principles that they support, you can begin to create your own class plans or find activities to meet your students' current needs. While these sample sessions are broken out by age, here are some examples:

	NEW CLASS with Community Theme Grades K-8 45 minutes	PRESCHOOL with Community Theme Ages 3-5 20 - 25 minutes	STRENGTH THEME Grades K-12 40 minutes	WILDLIFE LESSON with Stillness Theme Grades K-6 40 - 45 minutes
CALM	Belly Breathing with Hoberman Sphere	Hoberman Sphere Belly Breathing Demo Belly Breathing on back	Belly Breathing One-Minute Exploration: A time of strength	Belly Breathing 30-Second Stillness
	Roots Name Toss	Rock and Roll Boat	Woodchopper with Strong Voice	One-Minute Exploration: Travel to Alaska to photograph eagles
ACTIVE	Chair 15 Flow with focus on Warrior I	Star Pose	Witness each other's strength in Warrior I	Chair 15 Flow Eagle on a Rock
	Trust Walk	Galaxy (Star Circle) Tree Circle Trust Walk	Strong Voice	Archetype Game with Sneaky/Still Focus
CALM	Twist Relaxation Story that includes new friends	Back Drawing	Relaxation Story with visit to a strong person	Relaxation Story with facts about eagles

DISCIPLINING THE MIND with Listening Theme Grades 4-12 30 minutes	GROUNDING FOCUS Grades 2-12 40 - 45 minutes	TEST PREPARATION with Strength Theme Grades 2-12 25 - 30 minutes	ANXIETY with Grounding Theme Grades 1-12 30 - 40 minutes
Belly Breathing with Hoberman Sphere sitting in chairs	Forward Bend One-Minute Exploration: The life of a tree	Pinwheel Breath	Belly Breathing with Hoberman Sphere Pulse Count, one minute
One-Minute Exploration: Observe what's on minds followed by sharing	Roots	Arm Swings with positive self-talk	Roots Volcano Breath
Chair 15 Flow	Star Pose Galaxy (Star Circle)	Run in place one minute Pulse Count Roots (Mountain) Crescent Moon Dancer	Warrior I and II Tree for 30 seconds
Changing Channels	Tree Circle Tree Challenge	Shoulder Clock Tree with visualized support of loved one	Calm Voice Activity
One-Minute Exploration: A personal goal	Circle of Support	Twist One-Minute Exploration: A time you did something well	Back Drawing

CALM

⇩

ACTIVE

⇩

CALM

For help in designing your own class plans like these, see the instructions in Appendix C, Yoga Calm Lesson Planner (p.175).

Integrating Yoga Calm Activities into the Curriculum

Yoga Calm activities can be integrated in numerous ways with your school curricular objectives. For example, in reading classes, you can combine visualization and storytelling activities with a fairy-tale unit, or you can have individual students read calming stories to the class. You can use a kinesthetic activity such as Sensory Adventure or Back Drawing as a warm-up for a descriptive or imaginative writing assignment. Also for writing units, shared experiences help in developing word or idea banks. You can teach public speaking skills with "brain breaks," during which a student leads a favorite visualization or Back Drawing activity in front of the class.

For science classes, you can link all the physical work—poses and breathing activities—with lessons in physiology, anatomy, and health. Pinwheel Breath, partner poses, and the process of moving from Stillness to active processes can help introduce ideas about energy and motion. Similarly, in a math class, you can relate poses and motion to concepts such as symmetry, balance, and geometric shapes. You might even integrate an arithmetic lesson by practicing balance poses to the beat of a drum or rhythm sticks—for instance, holding Tree for five counts of four to twenty beats of the drum, then trying again with threes, twos, and so on.

Of course, you can work with the very basic matter of cooperative learning via a brief Community activity to bring together new study or work groups, as well as to develop trust.

These are just a few examples. The possibilities are endless. Let your own imagination soar!

Conclusion

On the last day of yoga for the school year, I asked the students if they wanted to continue the following year. The answer was a resounding Yes! When I asked why they felt it was important to continue, their responses varied. Several students said that yoga calmed them down and helped them relax. Maria, a fifth grader, said it helped her believe in herself, particularly at home when her family was fighting and yelling at one another. An active boy commented that it made him feel strong and it helped him with his basketball skills. And a boy who struggles with anxiety stated, "It helps me remember the good things in my life."

When working with children, we can always see how much they love the practice of self-study that yoga provides. Even more, the time spent in practice together gives them the meaningful and nurturing experiences they crave. They also appreciate the opportunities to relax and self-soothe. No doubt you will notice these same things develop in your own students as you begin to practice Yoga Calm with them.

When we teach workshops for teachers and other professionals we are moved by their skill, commitment, and creativity. And we are thrilled when they contact us later with stories of how adding this new dimension to their work, along with their own rich gifts and creativity, has deepened and enhanced their abilities in ways that have helped their students to blossom. We look forward to hearing your own stories as you integrate what you've learned here with the rest of your skills and knowledge, serving our future by working in service of children today.

Take what you've learned. Start slowly. Develop your yoga practice. Trust yourself. Use your imagination. And let us know how it goes.

The bud

Stands for all things,

even for those things that don't flower,

for everything flowers, from within, of self-blessing;

though sometimes it is necessary

to reteach a thing its loveliness,

to put a hand on the brow

of the flower

and retell it in words and in touch

it is lovely

until it flowers again from within, of self-blessing. . . .

—Galway Kinnell

Appendix A
Yoga Calm Curriculum Recommendations for Classroom Teachers

General Recommendations

- Begin with simple activities and hold poses for short times, as outlined below. Increase times as students develop abilities.

- Plan classes to make them interesting, while still keeping to the routine.

- Yoga Calm activities are most effective if they are done at the same time every day.

- If possible, schedule a special time once a week for longer activities.

- It may be useful to give the yoga time a special name—or just call it Yoga Calm time.

- Post the Ground Rules (p. 42) and have students use positive self-talk.

Stillness

Daily

- Practice a minimum of 30 seconds of quiet listening. Increase to 1 to 3 minutes as students show readiness (One-Minute Explorations and Guided Relaxations).

- Practice Belly Breathing with the Hoberman Sphere for a minimum of 30 seconds. As students are ready, allow them to lead.

- After students have practiced Belly Breathing for 2 to 3 weeks, instruct them on nose breathing and its benefits. Practice nose breathing daily and review the benefits once a month.

Three times a week

- Practice Pulse Count a minimum of 15 seconds. Increase time to 1 minute as students demonstrate ability. Instruct students on keeping their minds focused on their pulse for a full minute. Older students can challenge themselves by focusing for longer times.

Listening

General

- Before an active pose such as Warrior or Chair, or a balance pose, ask students to think of someone they want to be strong for. Allow them to share.

Once or twice a week

- Lead a One-Minute Exploration, asking students to tune in to how they are feeling.

- Lead Volcano Breath, allowing students to share.

To introduce later

- Lead Strong Voice and Calm Voice activities within the first few months. Display messages from these activities in the classroom.

Grounding

Daily

- Practice standing Activated in Mountain. This is the basis for all other physical poses.

Once or twice a week

- Demonstrate Woodchopper and describe the benefits. Occasionally review the benefits by asking students to repeat them.
- Practice Roots activity.
- Practice a balance pose, starting with either Tree or Modified Dancer. At first have students hold for 10 seconds. Increase time as they show readiness. Allow individual students to lead.

Strength

General

- Teach the phrases "I am strong. I am in control. I can do it. I can be responsible." Post the phrases in the classroom.
- Increase holding times for the poses as students are ready and ask individual students to lead.

Once or twice a week

- Practice a balance pose using the phrases above.
- Lead Warrior I, Warrior II, Chair, and one of the Basic Classroom Plans or flows in chapter 9.

Community

Once or twice a week

- Practice partner poses such as Shoulder Clock, Partner Pull, and Tree Challenge.

Weekly

- Practice a social/emotional activity, beginning with Trust Walk, Exploring Feelings, and Strong Voice. Repeat these or add new games as students are ready.
- Practice giving and receiving compliments (Compliment Game).

Monthly

- Play a challenging community game such as Tree Challenge or Tree Circle with challengers. Discuss challenges students encounter in friendships and community.

Sample Three-Week Lesson Plan

This plan can be adapted for various grades, K-8.

Week One

- **Monday:** Belly Breathing with Hoberman Sphere, Pulse Count, Twist, One-Minute Exploration on vacation theme
- **Tuesday:** Belly Breathing with Hoberman Sphere, Pulse Count, Mountain, Warrior I, Twist, One-Minute Exploration on feelings in body
- **Wednesday:** Belly Breathing with Hoberman Sphere, Pulse Count, Roots, Mountain, Tree, One-Minute Exploration on a time the student felt happy
- **Thursday:** Belly Breathing with Hoberman Sphere, Pulse Count, Mountain, Warrior I, Strong Voice, Twist, One-Minute Exploration on supporters in your life
- **Friday:** Belly Breathing with Hoberman Sphere, Pulse Count, Woodchopper, Roots, Warrior, Twist, Compliment Game, One-Minute Exploration on a time when someone gave you a compliment or you felt good about yourself

Week Two

- **Monday:** Introduce nose breathing and its benefits, Belly Breathing with Hoberman Sphere with nose breathing, one of the Basic Classroom Plans or flows in chapter 9, One-Minute Exploration
- **Tuesday:** One of the Basic Classroom Plans or flows in chapter 9, One-Minute Exploration
- **Wednesday:** One of the Basic Classroom Plans or flows in chapter 9, Trust Walk
- **Thursday:** Belly Breathing with Hoberman Sphere, Pulse Count with longer hold, instruction on focusing, Roots, Mountain, Tree using focusing techniques, One-Minute Exploration on a time you had to be very focused (give examples)
- **Friday:** Belly Breathing with Hoberman Sphere, One-Minute Exploration on current feelings in body, Exploring Feelings, Compliment Game

Week Three

- **Monday:** One of the Basic Classroom Plans or flows in chapter 9, One-Minute Exploration
- **Tuesday:** Belly Breathing with Hoberman Sphere, Roots, Mountain, Tree, Tree Circle without challengers, One-Minute Exploration on a time when you were supported
- **Wednesday:** Belly Breathing with Hoberman Sphere, Pulse Count with longer holding time, Roots with eyes shut, Tree with eyes shut, Tree Circle with challenge, One-Minute Exploration on a time someone challenged you and you stood up for yourself
- **Thursday:** Belly Breathing with Hoberman Sphere, Mountain, Woodchopper, Chair, Trust Walk/Sensory Adventure, One-Minute Exploration on a time when a friend showed you something new
- **Friday:** Belly Breathing with Hoberman Sphere, Pulse Count, Mountain, Upward Mountain & Crescent Moon, Tree, Tree Challenge without support of group and follow by asking students to share how they prevented being knocked down; display responses in classroom

Recommendations for Specific Circumstances

Use one or more activities for each circumstance.

Transitions

- Belly Breathing with Hoberman Sphere
- One-Minute Exploration
- 30 seconds of complete stillness
- Pulse Count for 30 seconds to 1 minute
- Chair Twist
- Balance poses such as Tree or Modified Dancer
- Have two or three students compliment the class on a transition that goes well

Before a Test

- Belly Breathing with Hoberman Sphere
- Roots
- Balance pose, imagining support from a family member
- Volcano Breath, imagining something you can bring into your day
- Quick 5 or Top 10 Basic Classroom Plan from chapter 9
- One-Minute Exploration, imagining doing well on the test
- Strong Voice or Calm Voice
- Pinwheel Breath

Upset Student

- Belly Breathing with Hoberman Sphere
- Reduce sensory input
- Allow the student to lie or sit down until the body calms down
- Child pose
- Allow the student to lie on his or her belly and under a blanket
- Pinwheel Breath
- Calm Voice
- Place your hand on the middle of the student's back
- Model slow, deep breathing to remain calm and stable for the student
- Reflect feelings and body signals to the student
- Ask the student to listen inside to see what is happening in his or her heart and mind
- Allow student to express his or her feelings and sensations verbally or through writing
- One-Minute Exploration, allowing the student to imagine a solution to the situation
- Refer student to school counselor to process the episode

Anxiety

- Belly Breathing with Hoberman Sphere
- Child pose
- Back Drawing
- Back Breathing
- Pinwheel Breath
- Twist
- Forward Bend, standing, with knees bent
- Balance pose with a focal point and imagining a person of support helping
- Strong Voice
- Calm Voice
- Long relaxation taking them to a peaceful or safe place
- Allow the student to lie on his or her belly and under a blanket
- Arm Swings with positive self-talk

Lethargy

- Woodchopper
- Upward Mountain
- Standing balance poses
- Warrior I and II
- Chair pose
- Pinwheel Breath
- One of the Basic Classroom Plans or flows in chapter 9
- One-Minute Exploration
- Arm Swings with positive self-talk
- Twist

Appendix

Yoga Calm Activity and Principle Index

B

	Page Number	Stillness	Listening	Grounding	Strength	Community
Activate/Relax Walk	58	X	X		X	X
Alternate Arm/Leg Kicks	59			X	X	
Archetype Game	105		X		X	X
Arm Swings	60			X	X	X
Back Breathing	61	X	X	X		X
Back Drawing	62	X	X			X
Belly Breathing	63	X	X	X		X
Block Creek	64			X		X
Boat	65			X	X	
Bow	66			X	X	
Bridge	67			X	X	
Calm Voice	106	X	X		X	X
Cat/Cow	68	X		X	X	
Chair	69			X	X	
Changing Channels	108	X	X		X	

	Page Number	Stillness ☽	Listening ♥	Grounding ▲	Strength ◉	Community 🌐
Child	70	X	X	X		
Cobra	71			X	X	
Communication Game	109		X			X
Community Circle	110	X	X			X
Compliment Game	112		X			X
Conflicting Feelings	113		X		X	X
Dancer	72	X		X	X	
Dolphin	73			X	X	
Downward Dog	74	X		X	X	
Eagle	75	X		X	X	
Exploring Feelings	114		X			X
Forward Bend	76	X	X	X		
Happiness Recipe	115		X			X
Harassment Prevention	117			X	X	X
Leg Extensions / Foot Circles	77			X		
Mat Tag	78				X	X
Mindful Snack	118	X				X
Mountain	79			X	X	
Partner Pull	80			X	X	X
Past, Present, and Future	119		X	X	X	X
Personal Space	121		X			X
Pinwheel Breath	81	X	X			
Plank	82			X	X	

	Page Number	Stillness	Listening	Grounding	Strength	Community
Pulse Count	83	X	X			
Rock and Roll	84			X	X	
Roots	85	X	X	X		
Shoulder Clock	86			X	X	X
Side Angle	87			X	X	
Star	88			X	X	
Strong Voice	122		X	X	X	X
Superman	89			X	X	
Table	90			X	X	
Tree	91	X		X	X	
Tree Challenge	92			X	X	X
Tree Circle	93			X	X	X
Triangle	94			X	X	
Trickster	124	X	X		X	X
Trust Walk / Sensory Adventure	126	X	X			X
Twist	95	X	X	X		
Upward Mountain / Crescent Moon	96			X	X	
Volcano Breath	97	X	X			X
Warrior I	98		X	X	X	
Warrior II	99		X	X	X	
Woodchopper	100			X	X	
Yes / No Game	127		X			X

Appendix | C
Yoga Calm Lesson Planner

Determine Your Theme

Determine your class goal(s), which could be to meet an academic objective, a Yoga Calm principle (e.g., Stillness, Listening, Grounding Strength or Community), a student/class need, or to explore a specific theme. If using a Yoga Calm principle as your theme, review Chapter 2.

Choose Your Activities

Review the activities in chapters 5, 6 and 7 or use the Activity and Principle Index in Appendix B to determine which activities support the theme or Yoga Calm principle on which you will be developing your lesson plan. For example, in developing a lesson plan with Grounding as the theme, you could, 1) help students become more aware of their physical connection to the earth through standing and balance poses, 2) develop awareness of social support in Tree Circle and 3) use relaxation processes and stories that give them a sense of being physically present and "grounded" in their bodies and safe.

Sequence Your Lesson

Sequence your selected activities into a lesson plan. This can be done in a variety of ways to suit your particular teaching context, but the overall approach is to get students focused and self aware, get them moving to activate their bodies and minds, teach them social/emotional or academic lessons, and then provide an activity or process that allows them to rest, reflect and integrate what they have learned. Here is a depiction of this approach:

CALM ⇨ ACTIVE ⇨ CALM

The sample lesson plans on pages 160-161 illustrate this approach.

Practice with Thematic Language

Note the words and language you highlighted from your personal Principle Inquiry Process worksheet (Chapter 2) and see how you might adapt them for your students' age/developmental level and weave them into your lesson plan instructions for that principle. Then, run through your lesson plan a few times to get a sense of timing and how to use your language and experience of that theme in your teaching.

Teach Your Lesson and Revise

Teach your lesson and make a log with your notes in it (e.g., what worked and what didn't, what language was effective with your students, etc.). Revise your plan and teach it again. Having ready-made lesson plans and short sequences for all five Yoga Calm Principles, common academic or therapeutic themes and other topical themes will be a great resource.

Sample Stillness Lesson Plan

Date: February 1, 2009   **Class:** 5th Grade Classroom
Teacher: Lynea Gillen

Yoga Calm Principle/Lesson Goal: Stillness

LESSON PLAN

CALM

- *Belly Breathing* with Hoberman sphere 10 breaths.
  Shut your eyes and listen to the stillness for 30 seconds.

ACTIVE

- *Rock and Roll.*

- *Boat* – Be a very still boat on a lake waiting for the fish. You don't want to move a muscle.

- Roll to standing.

- *Mountain* – Can you be a beautiful strong mountain. Shut your eyes and imagine
  that it is snowing on you. Feel how peaceful the mountain is when it is snowing.

- Mountain to Mountain pose flow (middle section of *Mat 20*) three
  times with different leaders. Mind a moment of stillness during
  the poses, especially during warrior and plank poses.

- *Tree Pose* – Let the wind blow through your branches, then return
  to stillness. Feel the contrast between windy and still.

- *Changing Tree* – 4 beats of windy, 4 beats of stillness on each leg.

CALM

- Ask students to be completely still for 30 seconds.

- Have them imagine themselves sitting by a very still lake. A momma deer
  and her baby come to the lake for a drink of water. You have to be very still
  so you don't scare them away. Watch the mommy and baby deer as they
  drink water from the lake, then slowly walk back into the woods.

Sample Community Lesson Plan

Date: February 1, 2009   **Class:** Friendship Counseling Group
Teacher: Lynea Gillen

Yoga Calm Principle/Lesson Goal: Community

LESSON PLAN

CALM

- *Belly Breathing* with one student leading with Hoberman sphere and another counting off a selected number of breaths.
- *Read Mindful Moment Card:* "Take a moment to remember the names of all the people in your family. Think of aunts, uncles, grandmas and grandpas, brothers and sisters. Image them making a circle around you to help you when you are in need."

ACTIVE

- *Roots* – With body activated, and eyes closed, circle right and left. Notice how your feet help you to balance. What are you circling around?
- *Tree Prep* – Now image one of your family members or friends holding your right foot steadily to the ground. See if you can slowly lift your other foot off the floor. Switch sides.
- *Tree Circle* – Notice how your friends help to support you.
- *Tree* – Now by yourself feel that support as you come into tree pose by yourself.

CALM

- *Community Circle* writing activity.
- Individual sharing and group discussion of who are your supporters in your life.
- Read *On the Day You Were Born* Story.

Sample Grounding Lesson Plan

Date: February 1, 2009   **Class:** 5th Grade Classroom
Teacher: Lynea Gillen

Yoga Calm Principle/Lesson Goal: Grounding

LESSON PLAN

CALM

- Belly Breathing on back, feeling the weight of your body on the floor. Make your legs heavy, feel the gravity holding you to the earth. Picture a solid rock that goes deep into the earth and imagine how heavy that rock is.

- Pulse Count – Find your pulse, then listen to the rhythm of your heart. Picture a big drum with a large stick and each time you hear your heart beat, imagine playing that big deep note on the drum. Play that drum for 20 beats of your heart.

ACTIVE

- *Rock and Roll* – Push your low back into the earth as you rock forward and back.

- *Boat* – Press down your sits bones and lift up through your heads.

- *Volcano Breath* – Imagine your breath rising up deep from the earth, like a volcano.

- *Mountain Pose* – Feel your feet rooted to the ground, heavy and grounded.

- Mountain to Mountain pose flow (middle section of *Mat 20*) three with a focus on holding the poses for a 8 count to help your body feel strong and grounded.

- Stand in a circle – *Roots* activity – feeling yourself anchored to the ground.

- With your eyes shut think of all people in your world who help you feel safe. Imagine them holding your feet to the ground.

- Practice *Trees in a Circle* activity to the count of 10 on each foot. Feel how your partner's support helps you to root your foot into the earth.

CALM

- *Relaxation* – Read the following Mindful Moment Card on Grounding: "Think of your favorite tree. Now imagine that you can plant that tree in a special place. Go to that place, dig a big hole and plant the tree. Imagine that you can see into the future and watch the tree grow tall."

Bibliography

Breath

Calais-Germain, B. (1993). *Anatomy of movement*. Seattle: Eastland.

Farhi, D. (1996). *The breathing book: Good health and vitality through essential breath work*. New York: Henry Holt.

Iyengar, B.K.S. (1995). *Light on pranayama: The yogic art of breathing*. New York: Crossroad.

Education

Breslin, M. (2006, September 28). Workout for mind and body: Naperville Central tests notion that exercise makes learning easier. *Chicago Tribune*. Retrieved May 28, 2007, from http://www.johnratey.com/Articles/chicagotribuneworkout.doc.

Bridgest, S., McCray, A.D., Neal, L., & Webb-Johnson, G. (2003). The effects of African American movement styles on teachers' perceptions and reactions. *Journal of Special Education*, 37(1), 49-57.

Campbell, D.G., & Brewer, C. (1991). *Rhythms of learning: Creative tools for developing lifelong skills*. Tucson: Zephyr.

Gardner, H. (1983). *Frames of mind: The theory of multiple intelligences*. New York: Basic.

Gardner, H. (1991). *The unschooled mind: How children think and how schools should teach*. New York: Basic.

Jensen, E. (1998). *Teaching with the brain in mind*. Alexandria, VA: Association for Supervision & Curriculum Development.

Manjunath, N.K., & Telles, S. (2004). Spatial and verbal memory test scores following yoga and fine arts camps for school children. *Indian Journal of Physiology and Pharmacology*, 48(3), 353-356.

Promislow, S., & Levan, C. (2005). *Making the brain body connection: A playful guide to releasing mental, physical and emotional blocks to success*. Canada: Enhanced Learning & Integration.

Ratey, J. (2003). *A user's guide to the brain*. United Kingdom: Time Warner Books UK.

Tough, P. (2006, November 26). What it takes to make a student. *New York Times Magazine*. Retrieved May 28, 2007, from http://www.nytimes.com/2006/11/26/magazine/26tough.html?ex=1182142800&en=f88b748bf061ed7e&ei=5087.

Psychology and Social Skills Training

Campbell, J. (1988). *The power of myth.* New York: Main Street (Doubleday).

Clance, P.R., Mitchell, M., & Engelman, S.R. (1980). Body cathexis in children as a function of awareness training and yoga. *Journal of Clinical Child Psychology, 9,* 82-85.

Goleman, D. (1995). *Emotional intelligence.* New York: Bantam.

Hyemeyohsts, S. (1983). *Song of Heyoehkah.* New York: Ballantine.

Jung, C.G. (1978). *Psychology and the East.* Princeton: Princeton University Press.

Kornblum, R. (2003). *Disarming the playground: Violence prevention through movement and pro-social skills.* Oklahoma City: Wood N Barnes.

Kornfield, J. (1993). *A path with heart: A guide through the perils and promises of spiritual life.* New York: Bantam.

Ladner, L. (2004). *The lost art of compassion.* New York: Harper Collins.

Linehan, M.M. (1993). *Skills training manual for treating borderline personality disorder.* New York: Guilford.

Lyubimov, N.N. (1999). Changes in electroencephalogram and evoked potentials during application of the specific form of physiological training (meditation). *Human Physiology, 25(1),* 171-180.

Seligman, M. (1996). *The optimistic child: Proven program to safeguard children from depression and build lifelong resilience.* New York: Harper.

Seligman, M. (2006). *Learned optimism.* New York: Vintage.

Stickgold, R., Hobson, J.A., Fosse, R., & Fosse, M. (2001, November 2). Sleep, learning, and dreams: Off-line memory reprocessing. *Science, 294(5544),* 1052-1057.

Relaxation

Benson, H., Wilcher, M., Greenberg, B., Huggins, E., Ennis, M., Zuttermeister, P.C., et al. (2000). Academic performance among middle-school students after exposure to a relaxation response curriculum. *Journal of Research and Development in Education, 33(3),* 156-165.

Clear your mind (2006). *NEA Today.* Retrieved May 28, 2007, from http://www.nea.org/neatoday/0605/upfront13.html.

Naiman, R. (2006). *Healing night.* Minneapolis: Syren.

Sipkin, D. (1985). Relaxation techniques for handicapped children: A review of literature. *Journal of Special Education, 19(3),* 283-289.

Stickgold, R., Hobson, J.A., Fosse, R., & Fosse, M. (2001, November 2). Sleep, learning, and dreams: Off-line memory reprocessing. *Science, 294(5544),* 1052-1057.

Stueck, M., & Gloeckner, N. (2005). Yoga for children in the mirror of the science: Working spectrum and practice fields of the training of relaxation with elements of yoga for children. *Early Child Development and Care, 175(4),* 371-377.

Telles, S., Narendran, S., Raghuraj, P., Nagarathna, R., & Nagendra, H.R. (1997). Comparison of changes in autonomic and respiratory parameters of girls after yoga and games at a community home. *Perceptual and Motor Skills, 84(1),* 251-257.

Travis, F., Tecce, J.J., & Guttman, J. (2000). Cortical plasticity, contingent negative variation, and transcendent experiences during practice of the Transcendental Meditation technique. *Biological Psychology, 55(1),* 41-55.

Sensory Integration

Ayres, J. (2005). *Sensory integration and the child.* Los Angeles: Western Psychological Services.

Kranowitz, Carol (2005). *The out-of-sync child: Recognizing and coping with sensory processing disorder.* New York: Berkley Publishing.

Trott, M.C., Laurel, M.K., & Windeck, S.L. (1993). *SenseAbilities: Understanding sensory integration.* San Antonio: Therapy Skill Builders.

Special Needs

Barkley, R. (1995). *Taking charge of ADHD: The complete authoritative guide for parents.* New York: Guilford.

Dendy, C.A.Z. (1995). *Teenagers with ADD.* Bethesda: Woodbine House.

Glass, R.M. (2000). Panic disorder—It's real and it's treatable. *Journal of the American Medical Association, 283,* 2573-2574.

Hallowell, E., & Ratey, J. (1994). *Driven to distraction.* New York: Touchstone.

Hill, R.W., & Castro, E. (2002). *Getting rid of Ritalin: How neurofeedback can successfully treat attention deficit disorder without drugs.* Charlottesville, VA: Hampton Roads.

Hopkins, J., Perlman, T., & Hechtman, L. (1979). Cognitive style in adults originally diagnosed as hyperactives. *Journal of Child Psychology and Psychiatry, 20*(3), 209-216.

Ingersoll, B. (1988). *Your hyperactive child: A parent's guide to coping with attention deficit disorder.* New York: Doubleday.

Jensen, P.S., & Kenny, D.T. (2004). The effects of yoga on the attention and behavior of boys with attention-deficit/hyperactivity disorder (ADHD). *Journal of Attention Disorders, 7,* 205 - 216.

Kelly, K., & Ramundo, P. (1993). *You mean I'm not lazy, stupid or crazy?: The classic self-help book for adults with attention deficit disorder.* New York: Scribner.

Kenney, M. (2002). Integrated movement therapy: Yoga-based therapy as a viable and effective intervention for autism spectrum and related disorders. International *Journal of Yoga Therapy, 12,* 71-79.

Klingberg, T., Fernell, E., Oleson, P.J., Johnson, M., Gustafsson, P., Dahlstrom, K., et al. (2005). Computerized training of working memory in children with ADHD—A randomized, controlled trial. *Journal of the American Academy of Child and Adolescent Psychiatry, 44*(2), 177-186.

Peck, H.L., Kehle, T.J., Bray, M.A., & Theodore, L.A. (2005). Yoga as an intervention for children with attention problems. *School Psychology Review, 34*(3), 415-424.

Reiff, M.I., & Tippins, S. (2004). *ADHD: A complete and authoritative guide.* Elk Grove Village, IL: American Academy of Pediatrics.

Rojas, N.L., & Chan, E. (2005). Old and new controversies in the alternative treatment of attention-deficit hyperactivity disorder. *Mental Retardation and Developmental Disability Research Reviews, 11*(2), 116-130.

Sipkin, D. (1985). Relaxation techniques for handicapped children: A review of literature. *Journal of Special Education, 19*(3), 283-289.

Slate, S.E., Meyer, T.L., Burns, W.J., & Montgomery, D.D. (1998). Computerized cognitive training for severely emotionally disturbed children with ADHD. *Behavior Modification, 22,* 415-437.

Solden, S. (1995). *Women with attention deficit disorder.* Nevada City, CA: Underwood.

Sousa, D.A. (2001). *How the special needs brain learns.* Thousand Oaks, CA: Corwin.

Sumar, S. (2001). *Yoga for the special child.* Evanston: Special Yoga Publications.

Tinius, T.P. & Tinius, K.A. (2000). Changes after EEG biofeedback and cognitive retraining in adults with mild traumatic brain injury and attention deficit hyperactivity disorder. *Journal of Neurotherapy,* 4(2), 27-44.

Warren, P., & Capehart, J. (1995). *You and your ADD child.* Nashville: Thomas Nelson.

Weiss, L. (1992). *Attention deficit disorder in adults.* Dallas: Taylor Trade.

Stress

Allen, J.S. , & Klein, R.J. (1986). *Ready…set…R.E.L.A.X.: A research-based program of relaxation, learning and self-esteem for children.* Watertown, WI: Inner Coaching.

Angus, S.F. (1989). Three approaches to stress management for children. *Elementary School Guidance and Counseling,* 22(3), 228-233.

Benn, R. (2004). Reduced stress, increased happiness among middle school students. Paper presented to the International Center for Integration of Health and Spirituality at the National Institutes of Health, Bethesda, MD.

Ornish, D. (1983). *Stress, diet and your heart.* New York: Henry Holt.

Sapolsky, R.M. (1994). *Why zebras don't get ulcers: The acclaimed guide to stress, stress-related diseases, and coping.* New York: Henry Holt.

Yoga and Movement

Coulter, D.H. (2001). *Anatomy of hatha yoga.* Honesdale, PA: Body and Breath.

Dennison, P.H., & Dennison, G.E. (1989). *Brain gym.* Ventura: Edu-Kinesthetics.

Espenak, L. (1981). *Dance therapy: Theory and application.* Springfield, IL: Charles C Thomas.

Farhi, D. (2000). *Yoga mind, body and spirit: A return to wholeness.* New York: Henry Holt.

Feuerstein, G. (2001). *The yoga tradition.* Prescott, AZ: Hohm.

Hannaford, C., & Pert, C.B. (2005). *Smart moves: Why learning is not all in your head.* Arlington, VA: Great Ocean.

Kalish, L., & Guber, T.L. (2002). *Yoga Ed.: Tools for teachers manual for grades K-8.* Los Angeles: YogaEd.

Kenney, M. (2002). Integrated movement therapy: Yoga-based therapy as a viable and effective intervention for autism spectrum and related disorders. *International Journal of Yoga Therapy,* 12, 71-79.

Lasater, J. (1995). *Relax and renew.* Berkeley: Rodmell.

Manjunath, N.K., & Telles, S. (2004). Spatial and verbal memory test scores following yoga and fine arts camps for school children. *Indian Journal of Physiology and Pharmacology,* 48(3), 353-356.

Mehta, M. (1994). *How to use yoga.* New York: Smithmark.

Peck, H.L., Kehle, T.J., Bray, M.A., & Theodore, L.A. (2005). Yoga as an intervention for children with attention problems. *School Psychology Review,* 34(3), 415-424.

Phillips, K., & Steward, M. (1992). *Yoga for children.* New York: Simon & Schuster.

Sexton, S. (2006, September–October). Yoga in schools: Does it pass the test? *Yoga + Joyful Living*. Retrieved May 28, 2007, from http://www.yogakids.com/news/200610-yoga-plus-joyful-living.html.

Slovacek, S.P., Tucker, S.A., & Pantoja, L. (2003). A study of the Yoga Ed program at the Accelerated School. Retrieved May 28, 2007, from http://www.yogaed.com/pdfs/researcharticle.pdf.

Stueck, M., & Gloeckner, N. (2005). Yoga for children in the mirror of the science: Working spectrum and practice fields of the training of relaxation with elements of yoga for children. *Early Child Development and Care*, 175(4), 371-377.

Sumar, S. (2001). *Yoga for the special child*. Evanston: Special Yoga Publications.

Telles, S., Hanumanthaiah, B., Nagarathna, R., & Nagendra, H.R. (1993). Improvement in static motor performance following yogic training of school children. *Perceptual and Motor Skills*, 76(3), 1264-1266.

Telles, S., Narendran, S., Raghuraj, P., Nagarathna, R., & Nagendra, H.R. (1997). Comparison of changes in autonomic and respiratory parameters of girls after yoga and games at a community home. *Perceptual and Motor Skills*, 84(1), 251-257.

Other Resources

Children's Books

De Brunhoff, L. (2002). *Babar's yoga for elephants*. New York: Abrams.

Frasier, D. (1991). *On the day you were born*. New York: Harcourt Brace.

Millman, D. (1992). *Secret of the peaceful warrior*. Tiburon, CA: Starseed.

Moser, A., & Pilkey, D. (1988). *Don't pop your cork on Mondays: The children's anti-stress book*. Kansas City: Landmark Editions.

Moser, A., & Melton, D. (1991). *Don't feed the monster on Tuesdays: The children's self-esteem book*. Kansas City: Landmark Editions.

Visit www.yogacalm.org to find Yoga Calm training opportunities and order these fine products to support your work with children.

Breathing Sphere

This is one of the most effective tools we have found for teaching relaxed, diaphragmatic breathing. Watching the sphere's three-dimensional action combined with the "belly breathing" calms, centers and relaxes children and adults alike.

Kids Teach Yoga, Flying Eagle DVD (ages 4 and up)

Through yoga, storytelling and beautiful footage of eagles in the wild, this award winning DVD creatively teaches children the qualities of the eagle - strength, focus and caring. Also includes focus and social skill activities for ADHD, a narrated science segment and beautiful HD nature footage.

Mindful Moments Cards

This beautifully illustrated deck of 50 short contemplations invite thoughtful reflection and self-awareness, and support social/emotional learning. Mindful Moments are a fun way for children to remember positive events in their lives, imagine successful futures and develop mindfulness, focus and relaxation skills.

Yoga Calm Posters

Reinforce Yoga Calm's wellness activities with these colorful and inspiring posters. This set of five 14" x 22" posters includes the Top 10, Chair 15 and Mat 20 routines as well as Ground Rules and Positive Thinking tips.

Heart of the Teacher - A guided yoga practice on Video DVD

From the loving support of our teachers and our community, we discover our gifts and are empowered to serve others. This timeless message from the yoga tradition is the touchstone for this 50 minute Hatha yoga class by Jim Gillen, RYT-500. Recorded live at a Yoga Calm Teacher Training, this DVD skillfully blends restorative yoga, energizing flows and lighthearted wisdom to inspire every student to blossom into their full potential.

Yoga Renewal - A guided yoga practice on Audio CD

Discover the ageless benefits of yoga with this 50 minute guided practice for beginning yoga students by Jim Gillen, RYT-500. Stretch and revitalize your entire body—taking the knots out of those tight shoulders, strengthening your back and abdomen, loosening up legs and hips and relaxing your mind.

Parenting ADD/ADHD Children DVD

Over the last 30 years, Dr. Jeff Sosne has helped thousands of children, teachers and families with ADD/ADHD issues. He is the author of two practical guides for parents and school personnel—*The ADHD Notebook* and *The Anger Notebook*—and co-teaches our ADHD workshops. This DVD includes Basic Principles, Behavior Management, Building Responsibility and Building Self Control.

Good People Everywhere

A soothing story to help children become mindful of the beautiful, caring people in their world. Each page delightfully unfolds with vibrant, engaging illustrations and endearing stories that warm hearts, evoke the imagination and inspire young and old alike to create a world of compassion and beauty. Winner of Mom's Choice, Theacher's Choice and Moonbeam Children's Book Awards.

Little Banty Chicken

A colorful picture book with an enchanting tale of one little chicken who has the courage to make her dream come true with the support of the wise moon and her barnyard friends.

Yoga Calm for Children - E-Book

Download this practical guide to teaching children yoga to your laptop, Kindle®, iPad® or other reading device. Over 100 color photographs and graphics! Check our website for special book/E-book bundles.

"This is truly an invaluable handbook that provides detailed and thoughtful information for counselors and teachers who want to incorporate the enormous benefits of yoga into a standard curriculum. It is also a beautiful expression of how, just by shifting the way we are with children, we can affect their lives."
—Frances Douglass, PhD School Psychologist

"This book resonates well with current physical education and recreation philosophies. Your strong multidisciplinary research coupled with you extensive background of working with children provides a strong foundation from which to present lesson plans that appeal to teachers and leaders who are striving to educate the whole child."
—Gayle Kassing, Ph.D.
Human Kinetics

"Yoga Calm is an extremely practical, useful, and well-conceived approach for addressing the diverse needs of both students and staff. I can genuinely recommend this book to other school districts."
—Howard Fetz, PhD
School District Superintendent

"This book does a wonderful job of integrating a complete mind/body/spirit/emotional approach with a first class section on the all-important information about social and emotional fluency. A book that also would be helpful to all parents as well as yoga teachers..."
—Ben Franklin Award Review Judge

"Yoga Calm is an excellent program that complements the services we provide for children. It reinforces the self-control principles we teach in our clinic and empowers the children and their families."
—Dr. Jeff Sosne, Director, The Children's Program and author of
The ADHD Notebook and *The Anger Notebook*

"Yoga is an important and often unused tool in the quest to offer children and teens protection from the negative effects of stress."
—Roger Klein, PsyD, Licensed Psychologist
Coauthor of *Ready, Set, RELAX*

"This book gives teachers and students a series of lessons for quieting and focusing bodies and minds for increased self-awareness and self-control. In the busyness of everyday life, this provides an opportunity for some purposeful slowing down and relaxation."
—Teachers Choice Award Judge

"This book beautifully illustrates how yoga techniques and philosophy can help children. The thoughtfully conceived exercises are accessible to teachers, counselors and students alike."
—Julie Gudmestad, Licensed Physical Therapist
Yoga Journal Columnist